Another Turn of the Crank

Another Turn of the Crank

Essays by

Wendell Berry

For Rollin Richmond
with good wishes

Wendell Berry
10/24/95

COUNTERPOINT
WASHINGTON, D.C.

Library of Congress Cataloging-in-Publication Data
Berry, Wendell, 1934–
    Another turn of the crank: essays / by Wendell Berry.
      1. Sustainable development.   2. Environmental policy.   3. Conservation of natural resources.
    I. Title.
    HC79.E5B459   1995
    333.7—dc20   95-31693
    ISBN 1-887178-03-1 (alk. paper)

FIRST PRINTING

Book design by David Bullen
Composition by Wilsted & Taylor
Printed in the United States of America on acid-free paper that meets the American National Standards Institute Z39-48 Standard.

COUNTERPOINT
P.O. Box 65793
Washington, D.C. 20035-5793

Distributed by Publishers Group West

For we are left but a few of many.

JEREMIAH 42:2

What to do? Stay green
Never mind the machine,
Whose fuel is human souls.
Live large, man, and dream small.

R. S. THOMAS

Contents

Foreword

THE ESSAYS in this book deal with a number of important issues that have now become obscured by poor politics, and they deal with other issues, equally important, that are now little noticed, and are perhaps not noticeable, by politicians; the book is therefore vulnerable to some misconceptions that I would like to correct beforehand.

Nothing that I have written here should be construed as an endorsement of either of our political parties as they presently function. Republicans who read this book should beware either of approving it as "conservative" or of dismissing it as "liberal." Democrats should beware of the opposite errors.

One reason for this is that I am an agrarian: I think that good farming is a high and difficult art, that it is indispensable, and that it cannot be accomplished except under certain conditions. Manifestly, good farming cannot be fostered or maintained under the rule of the presently dominant economic and cultural assumptions of our political parties.

Another reason is that I am a member, by choice, of a local community. I believe that healthy communities are indispensable, and I know that our communities are disintegrating under the influence of economic assumptions that are accepted without question by both our parties—despite their lip service to various noneconomic "values."

The "conservatives" believe that an economy that favors its richest and most powerful participants will yet somehow serve the best interest of everybody. The "liberals" believe just as irrationally that a merely competitive economy, growing always larger in scale and controlled by fewer and fewer people, can be corrected by extending government charity to the inevitable victims: the dispossessed, the unrepresented, and the unemployed. No agrarian or community member could look kindly upon or wish to serve either belief.

A reader would also be in error who concluded, from this book's reiterated wish to restore local life by means of local economies, that it is "antigovernment." On the contrary, one of the fundamental purposes of these essays is to serve the cause of democratic government as established by the Constitution. I do not believe, however, that a nation can secure such a government merely by means of a constitution. Political democracy can endure only as the guardian of economic democracy, as I am by no means the first to say. A democratic government fails in failing to protect the integrity of ordinary lives and local communities. By now it should be pretty obvious that central planning is of a piece with absentee ownership and does not work. But to say as much is not to say that there is no proper role for government. The proper role of a government is to protect its citizens and its communities against conquest—against economic conquest just as much as conquest by overt violence.

Underlying all that I have written here is the assumption that a people who are entirely lacking in economic self-determination, either personal or local, and who are therefore entirely passive in dealing with the suppliers of all their goods and services, including political goods and services, cannot be governed democratically—or not for long. This seems to be borne out by the present decline of political dialogue into a rhetoric of increasingly violent abstraction, without compassion, imagination, manners, or goodwill. The voter is no longer understood as an intelligent citizen to be persuaded, but rather as a benighted consumer requiring only to be distracted or deceived.

Furthermore, I am convinced that the present concentration of the best educated and most able people in centers of power, industry, and culture is a serious mistake. I believe that for many reasons—political, ecological, and economic—the best intelligence and talent should be at work and at home everywhere in the country. And therefore, my wishes for our schools are opposite to those of the present-day political parties and the present-day politics of education and culture. Wes Jackson has argued that our schools—to balance or replace their present single major in upward mobility—should offer a major in homecoming. I agree.

Finally, it would be an error to think that, because the arguments set forth in this book are not at present spoken or heard by any prominent politician, they are the work of a person thinking and writing in isolation. In fact, these essays belong to a conversation that is current, vigorous, and growing. There are now hundreds of organizations actively at work all over our country on behalf of local health, conservation, and economy.* The members of these organizations have been my teachers, they have given me hope, and I dedicate this book to them.

*For readers wishing to contact such organizations, help may be available from the Land Institute, 244 E. Water Well Road, Salina, KS 67401.

Acknowledgments

For help with these essays I am grateful to Tanya Berry, John M. Berry, Jr., Pam Clay, William H. Martin, Paula Huff, Marshall Pecore, Andy Cowart, Bill Herrick, Gurney Norman, Maurice Telleen, Wes Jackson, Brian Donahue, John Daniel, Jim Thomas, Philip Sherrard, Gary Anderson, Gene Logsdon, John Davis, Jack Shoemaker, and Nancy Palmer Jones.

Another Turn of the Crank

Farming and the Global Economy

WE HAVE BEEN repeatedly warned that we cannot know where we wish to go if we do not know where we have been. And so let us start by remembering a little history.

As late as World War II, our farms were predominantly solar powered. That is, the work was accomplished principally by human beings and horses and mules. These creatures were empowered by solar energy, which was collected, for the most part, on the farms where they worked and so was pretty cheaply available to the farmer.

However, American farms had not become as self-sufficient in fertility as they should have been—or many of them had not. They were still drawing, without sufficient repayment, against an account of natural fertility accumulated over thousands of years beneath the native forest trees and prairie grasses.

The agriculture we had at the time of World War II was nevertheless often pretty good, and it was promising. In many parts of our country we had begun to have established agricultural communities, each with its own local knowledge, memory, and tradition. Some of our farming practices had become well adapted to local conditions. The best traditional practices of the Midwest, for example, are still used by the Amish with considerable success in terms of both economy and ecology.

Now that the issue of sustainability has arisen so urgently, and in fact so transformingly, we can see that the correct agricultural agenda following World War II would have been to continue and refine the already established connection between our farms and the sun and to correct, where necessary, the fertility deficit. There can be no question, now, that that is what we should have done.

It was, notoriously, not what we did. Instead, the adopted agenda called for a shift from the cheap, clean, and, for all practical purposes, limitless energy of the sun to the expensive, filthy, and limited energy of the fossil fuels. It called for the massive use of chemical fertilizers to offset the destruction of topsoil and the depletion of natural fertility. It called also for the displacement of nearly the entire farming population and the replacement of their labor and good farming practices by machines and toxic chemicals. This agenda has succeeded in its aims, but to the benefit of no one and nothing except the corporations that have supplied the necessary machines, fuels, and chemicals—and the corporations that have bought cheap and sold high the products that, as a result of this agenda, have been increasingly expensive for farmers to produce.

The farmers have not benefited—not, at least, as a class—for as a result of this agenda they have become one of the smallest and most threatened of all our minorities. Many farmers, sad to say, have subscribed to this agenda and its economic assumptions, believing that they would not be its victims. But millions, in fact, have been its victims—not farmers alone but also their supporters and dependents in our rural communities.

The people who benefit from this state of affairs have been at pains to convince us that the agricultural practices and policies that have almost annihilated the farming population have greatly benefited the population of food consumers. But more and more consumers are now becoming aware that our supposed abundance of cheap and healthful food is to a considerable extent illusory. They are beginning to see that the social, ecological, and even the economic costs of such "cheap food" are, in fact, great. They are beginning to see that a system of food production that is dependent on massive applications of drugs and chemicals cannot, by definition, produce "pure food." And they are beginning to see that a kind of agriculture that involves unprecedented erosion and depletion of soil, unprecedented waste of water, and unprecedented destruction of the farm population cannot by any accommodation of sense or fantasy be called "sustainable."

From the point of view, then, of the farmer, the ecologist,

and the consumer, the need to reform our ways of farming is now both obvious and imperative. We need to adapt our farming much more sensitively to the nature of the places where the farming is done. We need to make our farming practices and our food economy subject to standards set not by the industrial system but by the health of ecosystems and of human communities.

The immediate difficulty in even thinking about agricultural reform is that we are rapidly running out of farmers. The tragedy of this decline is not just in its numbers; it is also in the fact that these farming people, assuming we will ever recognize our need to replace them, cannot be replaced anything like as quickly or easily as they have been dispensed with. Contrary to popular assumption, good farmers are not in any simple way part of the "labor force." Good farmers, like good musicians, must be raised to the trade.

The severe reduction of our farming population may signify nothing to our national government, but the members of country communities feel the significance of it—and the threat of it—every day. Eventually urban consumers will feel these things, too. Every day farmers feel the oppression of their long-standing problems: overproduction, low prices, and high costs. Farmers sell on a market that because of overproduction is characteristically depressed, and they buy their supplies on a market that is characteristically inflated—which is necessarily a recipe for failure, because farmers do not control either market. If they will not control production and if they will not reduce their dependence on purchased supplies, then they will keep on failing.

The survival of farmers, then, requires two complementary efforts. The first is entirely up to the farmers, who must learn—or learn again—to farm in ways that minimize their dependence on industrial supplies. They must diversify, using both plants and animals. They must produce, on their farms, as much of the required fertility and energy as they can. So far as they can, they must replace purchased goods and services with natural health and diversity and with their own intelligence. To increase production by increasing costs, as farmers have been doing for the last half century, is not only unintelligent; it is crazy. If farmers do not wish to cooperate any longer in their own destruction, then they will have to reduce their dependence on those global economic forces that intend and approve and profit from the destruction of farmers, and they will have to increase their dependence on local nature and local intelligence.

The second effort involves cooperation between local farmers and local consumers. If farmers hope to exercise any control over their markets, in a time when a global economy and global transportation make it possible for the products of any region to be undersold by the products of any other region, then they will have to look to local markets. The long-broken connections between towns and cities and their surrounding landscapes will have to be restored. There is much promise and much hope in such a restoration. But farmers must understand that this requires an economics of cooperation rather than competition. They must understand also that such an economy sooner or later will require some rational means of production control.

If communities of farmers and consumers wish to promote a sustainable, safe, reasonably inexpensive supply of good food, then they must see that the best, the safest, and most dependable source of food for a city is not the global economy, with its extreme vulnerabilities and extravagant transportation costs, but its own surrounding countryside. It is, in every way, in the best interest of urban consumers to be surrounded by productive land, well farmed and well maintained by thriving farm families in thriving farm communities.

If a safe, sustainable local food economy appeals to some of us as a goal that we would like to work for, then we must be careful to recognize not only the great power of the interests arrayed against us but also our own weakness. The hope for such a food economy as we desire is represented by no political party and is spoken for by no national public officials of any consequence. Our national political leaders do not know what we are talking about, and they are without the local affections and allegiances that would permit them to learn what we are talking about.

But we should also understand that our predicament is not without precedent; it is approximately the same as that of the proponents of American independence at the time of the Stamp Act—and with one difference in our favor: in order to do the work that we must do, we do not need a national organization. What we must do is simple: we must shorten the distance that our food is transported so that we are eating more and more from local supplies, more and more to the benefit of local farmers, and more and more to the satisfaction of local consumers. This can be done by cooperation among small organizations: conservation groups, churches, neighborhood associations, consumer co-ops, local merchants, local independent banks, and organizations of small farmers. It also can be done by cooperation between individual producers and consumers. We should not be discouraged to find that local food economies can grow only gradually; it is better that they should grow gradually. But as they grow they will bring about a significant return of power, wealth, and health to the people.

One thing at least should be obvious to us all: the whole human population of the world cannot live on imported food. Some people somewhere are going to have to grow the food. And wherever food is grown the growing of it will raise the same two questions: How do you preserve the land in use? And how do you preserve the people who use the land?

The farther the food is transported, the harder it will be to answer those questions correctly. The correct answers will not come as the inevitable by-products of the aims, policies, and procedures of international trade, free or unfree. They cannot be legislated or imposed by international or national or state agencies. They can only be supplied locally, by skilled and highly motivated local farmers meeting as directly as possible the needs of informed local consumers.

Conserving Communities

In October of 1993, the *New York Times* announced that the United States Census Bureau would "no longer count the number of Americans who live on farms." In explaining the decision, the *Times* provided some figures as troubling as they were unsurprising. Between 1910 and 1920, we had 32 million farmers living on farms—about a third of our population. By 1950, this population had declined, but our farm population was still 23 million. By 1991, the number was only 4.6 million, less than 2 percent of the national population. That is, our farm population had declined by an average of almost half a million people a year for forty-one years. Also, by 1991, 32 percent of our farm managers and 86 percent of our farmworkers did *not* live on the land they farmed.

These figures describe a catastrophe that is now virtually complete. They announce that we no longer have an agricultural class that is, or that can require itself to be, recognized by the government; we no longer have a "farm vote" that is going to be of much concern to politicians. American farmers, who over the years have wondered whether or not they counted, may now put their minds at rest: they do not count. They have become statistically insignificant.

We must not fail to appreciate that this statistical insignificance of farmers is the successful outcome of a national purpose and a national program. It is the result of great effort and of principles rigorously applied. It has been achieved with the help of expensive advice from university and government experts, by the tireless agitation and exertion of the agribusiness corporations, and by the renowned advantages of competition—of our farmers among themselves and with farmers of other countries. As a result, millions of country people have been liberated from farming, landownership, self-employment, and other idiocies of rural life.

But what has happened to our agricultural communities is not exceptional any more than it is accidental. This is simply the way a large, exploitive, absentee economy works. For example, here is a *New York Times* News Service report on "rape-and-run" logging in Montana:

> Throughout the 1980s, the Champion International Corp. went on a tree-cutting binge in Montana, leveling entire forests at a rate that had not been seen since the cut-and-run logging days of the last century.
>
> Now the hangover has arrived. After liquidating much

of its valuable timber in the Big Sky country, Champion
is quitting Montana, leaving behind hundreds of unemployed mill workers, towns staggered by despair and more
than 1,000 square miles of heavily logged land.

The article goes on to speak of the revival of "a century-
old complaint about large, distant corporations exploiting
Montana for its natural resources and then leaving after the
land is exhausted." And it quotes a Champion spokesman,
Tucker Hill, who said, "We are very sympathetic to those
people and very sad. But I don't think you can hold a company's feet to the fire for everything they did over the last
twenty years."

If you doubt that exhaustion is the calculated result of
such economic enterprise, you might consider the example
of the mountain counties of eastern Kentucky from which,
over the last three-quarters of a century, enormous wealth
has been extracted by the coal companies, leaving the land
wrecked and the people poor.

The same kind of thing is now happening in banking. In
the county next to mine an independent local bank was recently taken over by a large out-of-state bank. Suddenly some
of the local farmers and small business people, who had been
borrowing money from that bank for twenty years and whose
credit records were good, were refused credit because they did
not meet the requirements of a computer in a distant city.
Old and once-valued customers now find that they are
known by category rather than character. The directors and
officers of the large bank clearly have reduced their economic
thinking to one very simple question: "Would we rather
make one big loan or many small ones?" Or to put it only a

little differently: "Would we rather support one large enterprise or many small ones?" And they have chosen the large over the small.

This economic prejudice against the small has, of course, done immense damage for a long time to small or family-sized businesses in city and country alike. But that prejudice has often overlapped with an industrial prejudice against anything rural and against the land itself, and this prejudice has resulted in damages that are not only extensive but also long-lasting or permanent.

As we all know, we have much to answer for in our use of this continent from the beginning, but in the last half century we have added to our desecrations of nature a deliberate destruction of our rural communities. The statistics I cited at the beginning are incontrovertible evidence of this. But so is the condition of our farms and forests and rural towns. If you have eyes to see, you can see that there is a limit beyond which machines and chemicals cannot replace people; there is a limit beyond which mechanical or economic efficiency cannot replace care.

I am talking here about the common experience, the common fate, of rural communities in our country for a long time. It has also been, and it will increasingly be, the common fate of rural communities in other countries. The message is plain enough, and we have ignored it for too long: the great, centralized economic entities of our time do not come into rural places in order to improve them by "creating jobs." They come to take as much of value as they can take, as cheaply and as quickly as they can take it. They are interested in "job creation" only so long as the jobs can be done more cheaply by humans than by machines. They are not interested in the good health—economic or natural or human—of any place on this earth. And if you should undertake to appeal or complain to one of these great corporations on behalf of your community, you would discover something most remarkable: you would find that these organizations are organized expressly for the evasion of responsibility. They are structures in which, as my brother says, "the buck never stops." The buck is processed up the hierarchy until finally it is passed to "the shareholders," who characteristically are too widely dispersed, too poorly informed, and too unconcerned to be responsible for anything. The ideal of the modern corporation is to be (in terms of its own advantage) anywhere and (in terms of local accountability) nowhere. The message to country people, in other words, is this: Don't expect favors from your enemies.

And that message has a corollary that is just as plain and just as much ignored: The governmental and educational institutions from which rural people should by right have received help have not helped. Rather than striving to preserve the rural communities and economies and an adequate rural population, these institutions have consistently aided, abetted, and justified the destruction of every part of rural life. They have eagerly served the superstition that all technological innovation is good. They have said repeatedly that the failure of farm families, rural businesses, and rural communities is merely the result of progress and efficiency and is good for everybody.

We are now pretty obviously facing the possibility of a

world that the supranational corporations, and the govern-
ments and educational systems that serve them, will control
entirely for their own enrichment—and, incidentally and inescapably, for the impoverishment of all the rest of us. This
will be a world in which the cultures that preserve nature and
rural life will simply be disallowed. It will be, as our experience already suggests, a postagricultural world. But as we now
begin to see, you cannot have a postagricultural world that
is not also postdemocratic, postreligious, postnatural—in
other words, it will be posthuman, contrary to the best that
we have meant by "humanity."

In their dealings with the countryside and its people, the
promotors of the so-called global economy are following a set
of principles that can be stated as follows. They believe that a
farm or a forest is or ought to be the same as a factory; that
care is only minimally necessary in the use of the land; that
affection is not necessary at all; that for all practical purposes
a machine is as good as a human; that the industrial standards
of production, efficiency, and profitability are the only standards that are necessary; that the topsoil is lifeless and inert;
that soil biology is safely replaceable by soil chemistry; that
the nature or ecology of any given place is irrelevant to the use
of it; that there is no value in human community or neighborhood; and that technological innovation will produce
only benign results.

These people see nothing odd or difficult about unlimited
economic growth or unlimited consumption in a limited
world. They believe that knowledge is property and is power,
and that it ought to be. They believe that education is job

training. They think that the summit of human achievement is a high-paying job that involves no work. Their public boast is that they are making a society in which everybody will be a "winner"—but their private aim has been to reduce radically the number of people who, by the measure of our historical ideals, might be thought successful: the independent, the self-employed, the owners of small businesses or small usable properties, those who work at home.

The argument for joining the new international trade agreements has been that there is going to be a one-world economy, and we must participate or be left behind—though, obviously, the existence of a one-world economy depends on the willingness of all the world to join. The theory is that under the rule of international, supposedly free trade, products will naturally flow from the places where they can be best produced to the places where they are most needed. This theory assumes the long-term safety and sustainability of massive international transport, for which there are no guarantees, just as there are no guarantees that products will be produced in the best way or to the advantage of the workers who produce them or that they will reach or can be afforded by the people who need them.

There are other unanswered questions about the global economy, two of which are paramount: How can any nation or region justify the destruction of a local productive capacity for the sake of foreign trade? And how can people who have demonstrated their inability to run national economies without inflation, usury, unemployment, and ecological devastation now claim that they can do a better job in running a global economy? American agriculture has demonstrated by its own ruination that you cannot solve economic problems just by increasing scale and, moreover, that increasing scale is almost certain to cause other problems—ecological, social, and cultural.

We can't go on too much longer, maybe, without considering the likelihood that we humans are not intelligent enough to work on the scale to which we have been tempted by our technological abilities. Some such recognition is undoubtedly implicit in American conservatives' long-standing objection to a big central government. And so it has been odd to see many of these same conservatives pushing for the establishment of a supranational economy that would inevitably function as a government far bigger and more centralized than any dreamed of before. Long experience has made it clear—as we might say to the liberals—that to be free we must limit the size of government and we must have some sort of home rule. But it is just as clear—as we might say to the conservatives—that it is foolish to complain about big government if we do not do everything we can to support strong local communities and strong community economies.

But in helping us to confront, understand, and oppose the principles of the global economy, the old political alignments have become virtually useless. Communists and capitalists are alike in their contempt for country people, country life, and country places. They have exploited the countryside with equal greed and disregard. They are alike even in their plea that it is right to damage the present in order to make "a better future."

The dialogue of Democrats and Republicans or of liberals and conservatives is likewise useless to us. Neither party is interested in farmers or in farming or in the good care of the land or in the quality of food. Nor are they interested in taking the best care of our forests. The leaders of these parties are equally subservient to the supranational corporations. Of this the North American Free Trade Agreement and the new revisions to the General Agreement on Tariffs and Trade are proof.

Moreover, the old opposition of country and city, which was never useful, is now more useless than ever. It is, in fact, damaging to everybody involved, as is the opposition of producers and consumers. These are not differences but divisions that ought not to exist because they are to a considerable extent artificial. The so-called urban economy has been just as hard on urban communities as it has been on rural ones.

All these conventional affiliations are now meaningless, useful only to those in a position to profit from public bewilderment. A new political scheme of opposed parties, however, is beginning to take form. This is essentially a two-party system, and it divides over the fundamental issue of community. One of these parties holds that community has no value; the other holds that it does. One is the party of the global economy; the other I would call simply the party of local community. The global party is large, though not populous, immensely powerful and wealthy, self-aware, purposeful, and tightly organized. The community party is only now coming aware of itself; it is widely scattered, highly diverse, small though potentially numerous, weak though latently power-ful, and poor though by no means without resources.

We know pretty well the makeup of the party of the global economy, but who are the members of the party of local com-munity? They are people who take a generous and neighborly view of self-preservation; they do not believe that they can survive and flourish by the rule of dog eat dog; they do not believe that they can succeed by defeating or destroying or selling or using up everything but themselves. They doubt that good solutions can be produced by violence. They want to preserve the precious things of nature and of human cul-ture and pass them on to their children. They want the world's fields and forests to be productive; they do not want them to be destroyed for the sake of production. They know you cannot be a democrat (small *d*) or a conservationist and at the same time a proponent of the supranational corporate economy. They believe— they know from their experi-ence— that the neighborhood, the local community, is the proper place and frame of reference for responsible work. They see that no commonwealth or community of interest can be defined by greed. They know that things connect— that farming, for example, is connected to nature, and food to farming, and health to food— and they want to preserve the connections. They know that a healthy local community cannot be replaced by a market or an entertainment industry or an information highway. They know that contrary to all the unmeaning and unmeant political talk about "job creation," work ought not to be merely a bone thrown to the otherwise unemployed. They know that work ought to be necessary; it ought to be good; it ought to be satisfying and dignifying to the people who do it, and genuinely useful and pleasing to the people for whom it is done.

The party of local community, then, is a real party with a real platform and an agenda of real and doable work. And it has, we might add, a respectable history in the hundreds of efforts, over several decades, to preserve local nature or local health or to sell local products to local consumers. Now such efforts appear to be coming into their own, attracting interest and energy in a way they have not done before. People are seeing more clearly all the time the connections between conservation and economics. They are seeing that a community's health is largely determined by the way it makes its living.

The natural membership of the community party consists of small farmers, ranchers, and market gardeners, worried consumers, owners and employees of small shops, stores, community banks, and other small businesses, self-employed people, religious people, and conservationists. The aims of this party really are only two: the preservation of ecological diversity and integrity, and the renewal, on sound cultural and ecological principles, of local economies and local communities.

So now we must ask how a sustainable local community (which is to say a sustainable local economy) might function. I am going to suggest a set of rules that I think such a community would have to follow. And I hasten to say that I do not consider these rules to be predictions; I am not interested in foretelling the future. If these rules have any validity, that is because they apply now.

If the members of a local community want their community to cohere, to flourish, and to last, these are some things they would do:

1. Always ask of any proposed change or innovation: What will this do to our community? How will this affect our common wealth?

2. Always include local nature—the land, the water, the air, the native creatures—within the membership of the community.

3. Always ask how local needs might be supplied from local sources, including the mutual help of neighbors.

4. Always supply local needs *first.* (And only then think of exporting their products, first to nearby cities, and then to others.)

5. Understand the unsoundness of the industrial doctrine of "labor saving" if that implies poor work, unemployment, or any kind of pollution or contamination.

6. Develop properly scaled value-adding industries for local products to ensure that the community does not become merely a colony of the national or global economy.

7. Develop small-scale industries and businesses to support the local farm and/or forest economy.

8. Strive to produce as much of the community's own energy as possible.

9. Strive to increase earnings (in whatever form) within the community and decrease expenditures outside the community.

10. Make sure that money paid into the local economy circulates within the community for as long as possible before it is paid out.

11. Make the community able to invest in itself by maintaining its properties, keeping itself clean (without dirtying some other place), caring for its old people, teaching its children.

12. See that the old and the young take care of one another. The young must learn from the old, not necessarily and not always in school. There must be no institutionalized "child care" and "homes for the aged." The community knows and remembers itself by the association of old and young.

13. Account for costs now conventionally hidden or "externalized." Whenever possible, these costs must be debited against monetary income.

14. Look into the possible uses of local currency, community-funded loan programs, systems of barter, and the like.

15. Always be aware of the economic value of neighborly acts. In our time the costs of living are greatly increased by the loss of neighborhood, leaving people to face their calamities alone.

16. A rural community should always be acquainted with, and complexly connected with, community-minded people in nearby towns and cities.

17. A sustainable rural economy will be dependent on urban consumers loyal to local products. Therefore, we are talking about an economy that will always be more cooperative than competitive.

These rules are derived from Western political and religious traditions, from the promptings of ecologists and certain agriculturists, and from common sense. They may seem radical, but only because the modern national and global economies have been formed in almost perfect disregard of community and ecological interests. A community economy is not an economy in which well-placed persons can make a "killing." It is not a killer economy. It is an economy whose aim is generosity and a well-distributed and safeguarded abundance. If it seems unusual to hope and work for such an economy, then we must remember that a willingness to put the community ahead of profit is hardly unprecedented among community business people and local banks.

How might we begin to build a decentralized system of durable local economies? Gradually, I hope. We have had enough of violent or sudden changes imposed by predatory interests outside our communities. In many places, the obvious way to begin the work I am talking about is with the development of a local food economy. Such a start is attractive because it does not have to be big or costly, it requires nobody's permission, and it can ultimately involve everybody. It does not require us to beg for mercy from our exploiters or to look for help where consistently we have failed to find it. By "local food economy" I mean simply an economy in which local consumers buy as much of their food as possible from local producers and in which local producers produce as much as they can for the local market.

Several conditions now favor the growth of local food economies. On the one hand, the costs associated with our present highly centralized food system are going to increase. Growers in the Central Valley of California, for example, can no longer depend on an unlimited supply of cheap water for irrigation. Transportation costs can only go up. Biotechnology, variety patenting, and other agribusiness innovations are intended not to help farmers or consumers but to extend and prolong corporate control of the food economy; they will increase the cost of food, both economically and ecologically.

On the other hand, consumers are increasingly worried about the quality and purity of their food, and so they would like to buy from responsible growers close to home. They would like to know where their food comes from and how it is produced. They are increasingly aware that the larger and more centralized the food economy becomes, the more vulnerable it will be to natural or economic catastrophe, to political or military disruption, and to bad agricultural practice.

For all these reasons, and others, we need urgently to develop local food economies wherever they are possible. Local food economies would improve the quality of food. They would increase consumer influence over production; consumers would become participatory members in their own food economy. They would help to ensure a sustainable, dependable supply of food. By reducing some of the costs associated with long supply lines and large corporate suppliers (such as packaging, transportation, and advertising), they would reduce the cost of food at the same time that they would increase income to growers. They would tend to improve farming practices and increase employment in agriculture. They would tend to reduce the size of farms and increase the number of owners.

Of course, no food economy can be, or ought to be, *only* local. But the orientation of agriculture to local needs, local possibilities, and local limits is indispensable to the health of both land and people, and undoubtedly to the health of democratic liberties as well.

For many of the same reasons, we need also to develop local forest economics, of which the aim would be the survival and enduring good health of both our forests and their dependent local communities. We need to preserve the native diversity of our forests as we use them. As in agriculture, we need local, small-scale, nonpolluting industries (sawmills, woodworking shops, and so on) to add value to local forest products, as well as local supporting industries for the local forest economy.

As support for sustainable agriculture should come most logically from consumers who consciously wish to keep eating, so support for sustainable forestry might logically come from loggers, mill workers, and other employees of the forest economy who consciously wish to keep working. But *many* people have a direct interest in the good use of our forests: farmers and ranchers with woodlots, all who depend on the good health of forested watersheds, the makers of wood products, conservationists, and others.

What we have before us, if we want our communities

to survive, is the building of an adversary economy, a system of local or community economies within, and to protect against, the would-be global economy. To do this, we must somehow learn to reverse the flow of the siphon that has for so long been drawing resources, money, talent, and people out of our countryside with very little if any return, and often with a return only of pollution, impoverishment, and ruin. We must figure out new ways to fund, at affordable rates, the development of healthy local economies. We must find ways to suggest economically—for finally no other suggestion will be effective—that the work, the talents, and the interest of our young people are needed at home.

Our whole society has much to gain from the development of local land-based economies. They would carry us far toward the ecological and cultural ideal of local adaptation. They would encourage the formation of adequate local cultures (and this would be authentic multiculturalism). They would introduce into agriculture and forestry a sort of spontaneous and natural quality control, for neither consumers nor workers would want to see the local economy destroy itself by abusing or exhausting its sources. And they would complete at last the task of freedom from colonial economics begun by our ancestors more than two hundred years ago.

Conserving Forest
Communities

*Delivered as a speech at the Kentucky Forest Summit (in
conjunction with the Nineteenth Governor's Conference
on the Environment) at Louisville, Kentucky, September
29, 1994.*

I LIVE IN Henry County, near the lower end of
the Kentucky River Valley, on a small farm that is half woodland. Starting from my back door, I could walk for days and
never leave the woods except to cross the roads. Though
Henry County is known as a farming county, 25 percent of it
is wooded. From the hillside behind my house I can see thousands of acres of trees in the counties of Henry, Owen, and
Carroll.

Most of the trees are standing on steep slopes of the river

and creek valleys that were cleared and plowed at intervals from the early years of settlement until about the time of World War II. These are rich woodlands nevertheless. The soil, though not so deep as it once was, is healing from agricultural abuse and, because of the forest cover, is increasing in fertility. The plant communities consist of some cedar and a great diversity of hardwoods, shrubs, and wildflowers.

The history of these now-forested slopes over the last two centuries can be characterized as a cyclic alternation of abuse and neglect. Their best hope, so far, has been neglect—though even neglect has often involved their degradation by livestock grazing. So far, almost nobody has tried to figure out or has even wondered what might be the best use and the best care for such places. Often the trees have been regarded merely as obstructions to row cropping, which, because of the steepness of the terrain, has necessarily caused severe soil losses from water erosion. If an accounting is ever done, we will be shocked to learn how much ecological capital this kind of farming required for an almost negligible economic return: thousands of years of soil building were squandered on a few crops of corn or tobacco.

In my part of Kentucky, as in other parts, we never developed a local forest economy, and I think this was because of our preoccupation with tobacco. In the wintertime when farmers in New England, for example, employed themselves in the woods, our people went to their stripping rooms. Though in the earliest times we depended on the maple groves for syrup and sugar, we did not do so for very long. In this century, the fossil fuels weaned most of our households from firewood. For those reasons and others, we have never very consistently or very competently regarded trees as an economic resource.

And so as I look at my home landscape, I am happy to see that I am to a considerable extent a forest dweller. But I am unhappy to remember every time I look—for the landscape itself reminds me—that I am a dweller in a forest for which there is, properly speaking, no local forest culture and no local forest economy. That is to say that I live in a threatened forest.

Such woodlands as I have been describing are now mostly ignored so long as they are young. After the trees have reached marketable size, especially in a time of agricultural depression, the landowners come under pressure to sell them. And then the old cycle is repeated, as neglect is once more superseded by abuse. The salable trees are marked, and the tract of timber is sold to somebody who may have no connection, economic or otherwise, to the local community. The trees are likely to be felled and dragged from the woods in ways that do more damage than necessary to the land and the young trees. The skidder may take the logs straight upslope, leaving scars that (depending on how they catch the runoff) will be slow to heal or will turn into gullies that will never heal. There is no local *interest* connecting the woods workers to the woods. They do not regard the forest as a permanent resource but rather as a purchased "crop" that must be "harvested" as quickly and as cheaply as possible.

The economy of this kind of forestry is apt to be as deplorable as its ecology. More than likely only the prime log of each tree is taken—that is, the felled tree is cut in two below the first sizable branch, leaving many board feet in short logs (that would be readily usable, say, if there were small local woodworking shops) as well as many cords of firewood. The trees thus carelessly harvested will most likely leave the local community and the state as sawlogs or, at best, rough lumber. The only local economic benefit may well be the single check paid by the timber company to the landowner.

But the small landowners themselves may not receive the optimum benefit, for the prevailing assumptions and economic conditions encourage or require them to sell all their marketable trees at the same time. Unless the landowner is also a logger with the know-how and the means of cutting timber and removing it from the woods, the small, privately owned woodland is not likely to be considered a source of steady income, producing a few trees every year or every few years. For most such landowners in Kentucky, a timber sale may be thinkable only once or twice in a lifetime.

Furthermore, such landowners now must, as a matter of course, sell their timber on a market in which they have no influence, in which the power is held almost exclusively by the buyer. The sellers, of course, may choose not to sell—but only if they can *afford* not to sell. The private owners of Kentucky woodlands are in much the same fix that Kentucky tobacco producers were in before the time of the Burley Tobacco Growers Cooperative Association—and in much the same fix as most American farmers today. They cannot go to market except by putting themselves at the mercy of the market. This is a matter of no little significance and concern in a rural state in which 90.9 percent of the forestland "is owned by approximately 440,000 nonindustrial private owners, whose average holding is 26 acres."[1]

I have been describing one version of present-day commercial forestry in Kentucky—what might be called the casual version.

But we also have in view another version. This is the big-money, large-scale corporate version. It involves the building of a large factory in a forested region, predictably accompanied by political advertisements about "job creation" and "improving the local economy." This factory, instead of sawing trees into boards, will reduce them to pulp for making paper, or it will grind or shred them and make boards or prefabricated architectural components by gluing together the resulting chips or strands.

Obviously, there are some advantages to these methods. Pulping or shredding can certainly use more of a tree than, say, a conventional sawmill. The laminated-strand process can make good building material out of low-quality trees. And there is no denying our society's need for paper and for building materials.

But from the point of view of either the forest or the local human community, there are also a number of problems associated with this kind of operation.

The fundamental problem is that it is costly and large in scale. It is therefore beyond the reach of small rural communities and so will be run inevitably for the benefit not of the local people but of absentee investors. And because of its cost and size, a large wood-products factory establishes in the local forest an enormous appetite for trees.

The very efficiency of a shredding mill—its ability to use small or low-quality trees—necessarily predisposes it to clear-cutting rather than to selective and sustained production. And a well-known inclination of such industries is toward forest monocultures, which do not have the ecological stability of natural forests.

As Kentuckians know from plenty of experience, nonexploitive relationships between large industries and small communities are extremely rare, if they exist at all. A large industrial operation might conceivably be established upon the most generous and forbearing principles of forestry and with the most benevolent intentions toward the local people. But we must remember that this large operation involves a large investment. And experience has taught us that large investments tend to take precedence over ecosystems and communities. In a time of economic adversity, the community and the forest will be sacrificed before the factory will be. The ideal of such operations is maximum profit to the owners or shareholders, who are not likely to be members of the local community. This means what it has always meant: labor and materials must be procured as cheaply as possible, and real human and ecological costs must be "externalized"—charged to taxpayers or to the future.

And so Kentucky forestry, at present, is mainly of two kinds: the casual and careless logging that is hardly more than an afterthought of farming, and the large-scale exploitation of the forest by absentee owners of corporations. Neither kind is satisfactory, by any responsible measure, in a state whose major natural resources will always be its productive soils and whose landscape today is one-half forested.

Kentucky has 12,700,000 acres of forest—almost 20,000 square miles. Very little of this is mature forest; nearly all of the old-growth timber had been cut down by 1940. Kentucky woodlands are nevertheless a valuable economic resource, supporting at present a wood-products industry with an annual payroll of $300 million and employing about 25,000 people. In addition, our forestlands contribute significantly to Kentucky's attractiveness to tourists, hunters, fishermen, and campers. They contribute indirectly to the economy by protecting our watersheds and our health.

But however valuable our forests may be now, they are nothing like so valuable as they can become. If we use the young forests we have now in the best way and if we properly care for them, they will continue to increase in board footage, in health, and in beauty for several more human generations. But already we are running into problems that can severely limit the value and usefulness of this resource to our people, because we have neglected to learn to practice good forest stewardship.

Moreover, we have never understood that the only appropriate human response to a diversified forest ecosystem is a diversified local forest economy. We have failed so far to imagine and put in place the sort of small-scale, locally owned logging and wood-products industries that would be the best guarantors of the long-term good use and good care of our forests. At present, it is estimated that up to 70 percent of the timber production of our forests leaves the state as logs or as raw lumber.

Lest you think that the situation and the problems I have outlined are of interest only to "tree huggers," let me remind you that during most of the history of our state, our rural landscapes and our rural communities have been in bondage to an economic colonialism that has exploited and misused both land and people. This exploitation has tended to become more severe with the growth of industrial technology. It has been most severe and most obvious in the coalfields of eastern Kentucky, but it has been felt and has produced its dire effects everywhere. With few exceptions our country people, generation after generation, have been providers of cheap fuels and raw materials to be used or manufactured in other places and to the profit of other people. They have added no value to what they have produced, and they have gone onto the markets without protection. They have sold their labor, their mineral rights, their crops, their livestock, and their trees with the understanding that the offered price was the price that they must take. Except for the tobacco program and the coal miners' union, rural Kentuckians have generally been a people without an asking price. We have developed the psychology of a subject people, willing to take whatever we have been offered and to believe whatever we have been told by our self-designated "superiors."

Now, with the two staple economies of coal and tobacco in doubt, we ask, "What can we turn to?" This is a question for every Kentuckian, but immediately it is a question for the rural communities. It is a question we may have to hold before ourselves for a long time, because the answer is going to be complex and difficult. If, however, as a part of the answer, we say, "Timber," I believe we will be right.

But we must be careful. In the past we have too often merely trusted that the corporate economy or the government would dispose of natural resources in a way that would be best for the land and the people. I hope we will not do that again. That trust has too often been catastrophically misplaced. From now on we should disbelieve that any corporation ever comes to any rural place to do it good, to "create jobs," or to bring to the local people the benefits of the so-called free market. It will be a tragedy if the members of Kentucky's rural communities ever again allow themselves passively to be sold off as providers of cheap goods and cheap labor. To put the bounty and the health of our land, our only commonwealth, into the hands of people who do not live on it and share its fate will always be an error. For whatever determines the fortune of the land determines also the fortune of the people. If the history of Kentucky teaches anything, it teaches that.

But the peculiarity of our history, so far, is that we have not had to learn the lesson. When the Old World races settled here, they saw a natural abundance so vast they could not imagine that it could be exhausted or ruined. Because it was vast and because virtually a whole continent was opening to the west, many of our forebears felt free to use the land carelessly and to justify their carelessness on the assumption that they could escape what they ruined. That early regardlessness

of consequence infected our character, and so far it has dominated the political and economic life of our state. So far, for
every Kentuckian, like Harry Caudill, willing to speak of the
natural limits within which we have been living all along,
there have been many who have wished only to fill their pock-
ets and move on, leaving their ecological debts to be paid by
somebody else's children.

But by this time, the era of cut-and-run economics *ought*
to be finished. Such an economy cannot be rationally defended or even apologized for. The proofs of its immense
folly, heartlessness, and destructiveness are everywhere. Its
failure as a way of dealing with the natural world and human
society can no longer be sanely denied. That this economic
system persists and grows larger and stronger in spite of its ev-
ident failure has nothing to do with rationality or, for that
matter, with evidence. It persists because, embodied now
in multinational corporations, it has discovered a terrifying
truth: If you can control a people's economy, you don't need
to worry about its politics; its politics have become irrelevant.
If you control people's choices as to whether or not they will
work, and where they will work, and what they will do, and
how well they will do it, and what they will eat and wear, and
the genetic makeup of their crops and animals, and what they
will do for amusement, then why should you worry about
freedom of speech? In a totalitarian economy, any "political
liberties" that the people might retain would simply cease to
matter. If, as is often the case already, nobody can be elected
who is not wealthy, and if nobody can be wealthy without de-

pendence on the corporate economy, then what is your vote worth? The citizen thus becomes an economic subject.

A totalitarian economy might "correct" itself, of course, by a total catastrophe—total explosion or total contamination or total ecological exhaustion. A far better correction, however, would be a cumulative process by which states, regions, communities, households, or even individuals would begin to work toward economic self-determination and an appropriate measure of local independence. Such a course of action would involve us in a renewal of thought about our history and our predicament. We must ask again whether or not we really want to be a free people. We must consider again the linkages between land and landownership and land use and liberty. And we must ask, as we have not very seriously asked before, what are the best ways to use and to care for our land, our neighbors, and our natural resources.

If economists ever pay attention to such matters, they may find that as the scale of an enterprise increases, its standards become more and more simple, and it answers fewer and fewer needs in the local community. For example, in the summer of 1982, according to an article in *California Forestry Notes*, three men, using five horses, removed 400,780 board feet from a 35.5-acre tract in Latour State Forest.[2] This was a "thinning operation." Two of the men worked full time as teamsters, using two horses each; one man felled the trees and did some skidding with a single horse. The job required sixty-four days. It was profitable both for the state forest and for the operator. During the sixty-four days the skidders barked a total of eight trees, only one of which was damaged badly enough to require removal. Soil disturbance in the course of the operation was rated as "slight."

At the end of this article the author estimates that a tractor could have removed the logs two and a half times as fast as the horses. And thus he implies a question that he does not attempt to answer: Is it better for two men and four horses to work sixty-four days, or for one man and one machine to do the same work in twenty-five and a half days? Assuming that the workers would all be from the local community, it is clear that the community, a timber company, and a manufacturer of mechanical skidders would answer that question in different ways. The timber company and the manufacturer would answer on the basis of a purely economic efficiency: the need to produce the greatest volume, hence the greatest profit, in the shortest time. The community, on the contrary—and just as much as a matter of self-interest—might reasonably prefer the way of working that employed the most people for the longest time and did the least damage to the forest and the soil. The community might conclude that the machine, in addition to the ecological costs of its manufacture and use, not only replaced the work of one man but more than halved the working time of another. From the point of view of the community, it is *not* an improvement when the number of employed workers is reduced by the introduction of labor-saving machinery.

This question of which technology is better is one that our society has almost never thought to ask on behalf of the local community. It is clear nevertheless that the corporate standard of judgment, in this instance as in others, is radically oversimplified, and that the community standard is sufficiently complex. By using more people to do better work, the economic need is met, but so are other needs that are social and ecological, cultural and religious.

We can safely predict that for a long time there are going to be people in places of power who will want to solve our local problems by inviting in some great multinational corporation. They will want to put millions of dollars of public money into an "incentive package" to make it worthwhile for the corporation to pay low wages for our labor and to pay low prices for, let us say, our timber. It is well understood that nothing so excites the glands of a free-market capitalist as the offer of a government subsidy.

But before we agree again to so radical a measure, producing maximum profits to people who live elsewhere and minimal, expensive benefits to ourselves and our neighbors, we ought to ask if we cannot contrive local solutions for our local problems, and if the local solutions might not be the best ones. It is not enough merely to argue against a renewal of the old colonial economy. We must have something else competently in mind.

If we don't want to subject our forests to the rule of absentee exploiters, then we must ask what kind of forest economy we would like to have. By "we" I mean all the people of our state, of course, but I mean also, and especially, the people of our state's rural counties and towns and neighborhoods.

Obviously, I cannot speak for anybody but myself. But as a citizen of this state and a member of one of its rural communities, I would like to offer a description of what I believe would be a good forest economy. The following are not my own ideas, as you will see, but come from the work of many people who have put first in their thoughts the survival and the good health of their communities.

A good forest economy, like any other good land-based economy, would aim to join the local human community and the local natural community or ecosystem together as conservingly and as healthfully as possible.

A good forest economy would therefore be a local economy, and the forest economy of a state or region would therefore be a decentralized economy. The only reason to centralize such an economy is to concentrate its profits into the fewest hands. A good forest economy would be owned locally. It would afford a decent livelihood to local people. And it would propose to serve local needs and fill local demands first, before seeking markets elsewhere.

A good forest economy would preserve the local forest in its native diversity, quality, health, abundance, and beauty. It would recognize no distinction between its own prosperity and the prosperity of the forest ecosystem. A good forest economy would function in part as a sort of lobby for the good use of the forest.

A good forest economy would be properly scaled. Individual enterprises would be no bigger than necessary to ensure the best work and the best livelihood for workers. The ruling purpose would be to do the work with the least possible disturbance to the local ecosystem and the local human community. Keeping the scale reasonably small is good for the forest. Only a local, small-scale forest economy would permit, for example, the timely and selective logging of small woodlots.

Another benefit of smallness of scale is that it preserves economic democracy and the right of private property. Property boundaries, as we should always remember, are human conventions, useful for defining not only privileges but also responsibilities, so that use may always be accompanied by knowledge, affection, care, and skill. Such boundaries exist only because the society as a whole agrees to their existence. If the right of landownership is used only to protect an owner's wish to abuse or destroy the land, upon which the community's welfare ultimately depends, then society's interest in maintaining the convention understandably declines. And so in the interest of democracy and property rights, there is much to be gained by keeping especially the land-based industries small.

A good forest economy would be locally complex. People in the local community would be employed in forest management, logging, and sawmilling, in a variety of value-adding small factories and shops, and in satellite or supporting industries. The local community, that is, would be enabled by its economy to realize the maximum income from its local resource. This is the opposite of a colonial economy.

It would answer unequivocally the question, To *whom* is the value added?

Furthermore, a local forest economy, living by the measure of local economic health, might be led to some surprising alterations of logging technology. For example, it would almost certainly have to look again at the use of draft animals in logging. This would not only be kinder to the forest but would also be another way of elaborating the economy locally, requiring lower investment and less spending outside the community.

A good forest economy would make good forestry attractive to landowners, providing income from recreational uses of their woodlands, markets for forest products other than timber, and so on.

A good forest economy would obviously need to be much interested in local education. It would, of course, need to pass on to its children the large culture's inheritance of book learning. But also, both at home and in school, it would want its children to acquire a competent knowledge of local geography, ecology, history, natural history, and of local songs and stories. And it would want a system of apprenticeships, constantly preparing young people to carry on the local work in the best way.

All along, I have been implying that a good forest economy would be a limited economy. It would be limited in scale and limited by the several things it would not do. But it would be limited also by the necessity to leave some wilderness tracts of significant acreage unused. Because of its inclination to be proud and greedy, human character needs this practical deference toward things greater than itself; this is, I think, a religious deference. Also, for reasons of self-interest and our own survival, we need wilderness as a standard. Wilderness gives us the indispensable pattern and measure of sustainability.

To assure myself that what I have described as a good forest economy is a real possibility, I went to visit the tribal forest of the Menominee Indians in northern Wisconsin. In closing, I want to say what I learned about that forest—from reading; from talking with Marshall Pecore, the forest manager, and others; and from seeing for myself.

The Menominee originally inhabited a territory of perhaps ten million acres in Wisconsin and northern Michigan. By the middle of the nineteenth century, as the country was taken up by white settlers, the tribal holding had been reduced to 235,000 acres, 220,000 acres of which were forested.

The leaders understood that if the Menominee were to live, they would have to give up their old life of hunting and gathering and make timber from their forest a major staple of their livelihood; they understood also that if the Menominee were to survive as a people, they would have to preserve the forest while they lived from it. And so in 1854 they started logging, having first instituted measures to ensure that neither the original nature nor the productive capacity of the forest would be destroyed by their work. Now, 140 years later, Menominee forest management has become technically sophisticated, but it is still rooted in cultural tradition, and its goal has remained exactly the same: to preserve the identification of the human community with the forest, and to give an absolute priority to the forest's ecological integrity. The result, in comparison to the all-too-common results of land use in the United States, is astonishing. In 1854, when logging was begun, the forest contained an estimated billion and a half board feet of standing timber. No records exist for the first thirteen years, but from 1865 to 1988 the forest yielded two billion board feet. And today, after 140 years of continuous logging, the forest still is believed to contain a billion and a half board feet of standing timber. Over those 140 years, the average diameter of the trees has been reduced by only one half of one inch—and that by design, for the foresters want fewer large hemlocks.

About 20 percent of the forest is managed in even-aged stands of aspen and jack pine, which are harvested by clear-cutting and which regenerate naturally. The rest of the forest is divided into 109 compartments, to each of which the foresters return every fifteen years to select trees for cutting. Their rule is to cut the worst and leave the best. That is, the loggers remove only those trees that are unlikely to survive for another fifteen years, those that are stunted or otherwise defective, and those that need to be removed in order to improve the stand. Old trees that are healthy and still growing are left uncut. As a result, this is an old forest, containing, for example, 350-year-old hemlocks, as well as cedars that are probably older. The average age of harvested maples is 140 to 180 years.

In support of this highly selective cutting, the forest is kept under constant study and evaluation. And loggers in the forest are strictly regulated and supervised. Even though the topography of the forest is comparatively level, skidders must be small and rubber-tired. Loggers must use permanent skid trails. And all logging contractors must attend training sessions.

The Menominee forest economy currently employs—in forest management, logging, milling, and other work—215 tribe members, or nearly 16 percent of the adult population of the reservation. As the Menominee themselves know, this is not enough; the economy of the forest needs to be more diverse. Its products at present are sawed lumber, logs, veneer logs, pulpwood, and "specialty woods" such as paneling and moldings. More value-adding industries are needed, and the Menominee are working on the problem. One knowledge able observer has estimated that "they could probably turn twice the profit with half the land under management if they used more secondary processing."[3]

Kentuckians looking for the pattern of a good local forest economy would have to conclude, I think, that the Menominee example is not complex enough, but that in all other ways it is excellent. We have much to learn from it. The paramount lesson undoubtedly is that the Menominee forest economy is as successful as it is because it is not understood primarily as an economy. Everybody I talked to on my visit urged me to understand that the forest is the basis of a culture and that the unrelenting cultural imperative has been to keep the forest intact—to preserve its productivity and the diversity of its trees, both in species and in age. The goal has always been a diverse, old, healthy, beautiful, productive, community-supporting forest that is home not only to its wild inhabitants but also to its human community. To secure this goal, the Menominee, following the dictates of their culture, have always done their work bearing in mind the needs of the seventh generation of their descendants.

And so, to complete my description of a good forest economy, I must add that it would be a long-term economy. Our modern economy is still essentially a crop-year economy—as though industrialism had founded itself upon the principles of the worst sort of agriculture. The ideal of the industrial economy is to shorten as much as possible the interval separating investment and payoff; it wants to make things fast, especially money. But even the slightest acquaintance with the vital statistics of trees places us in another kind of world. A forest makes things slowly; a good forest economy would therefore be a patient economy. It would also be an unselfish one, for good foresters must always look toward harvests that they will not live to reap.

1. William H. Martin, Mark Matuszewski, Robert N. Muller, and Bradley E. Powell, "Kentucky's Forest Resources" (unpublished paper), 3. I have taken statistics and other information on Kentucky forests from this paper and also from William H. Martin, "Sustainable Forestry in Kentucky," *In Context* (Center for Economic Development at Eastern Kentucky University, winter 1993), 1, 5–6; and William H. Martin, "Characteristics of Old-

Growth Mixed Mesophytic Forests," *Natural Areas Journal* 12, no. 3 (July 1992): 127–135.

2. Dave McNamara, "Horse Logging at Latour," *California Forestry Notes* (Sept. 1983): 1–10.

3. Scott Landis, "Seventh-Generation Forestry," *Harrowsmith Country Life* (Nov./Dec. 1992): 33. I also made use of Marshall Pecore, "Menominee Sustained-Yield Management," *Journal of Forestry* (July 1992): 12–16.

Private Property and the Common Wealth

Delivered as a speech at a conference on "The Forest Commons" at Eastern Kentucky University, Richmond, Kentucky, March 31, 1995.

THIS ESSAY OWES its existence to anxiety and to insomnia. I write, as I must, from the point of view of a country person, a member of a small rural community that has been dwindling rapidly since the end of World War II. Only the most fantastical optimism could ignore the possibility that my community is doomed—that it was doomed by the overwhelming victory of industrialism over agrarianism (both North and South) in the Civil War and the history both subsequent and consequent to it. It may be that my community—its economy, its faith, its local knowledge, its affection

for itself and its place—will dwindle on for another generation or two and then disappear or be replaced by a com-
muters' suburb. If it is doomed, then I have no doubt that
much else is doomed also, for I cannot see how a nation, a society, or a civilization can live while its communities die.

If that were all my thought, then I might find some comfort in despair. I might resign myself and at least sleep better.
But I am convinced that the death of my community is not
necessary and not inevitable. I believe that such remnant
communities as my own, fallen to the ground as they are,
might still become the seeds of a better civilization than we
now have—better economy, better faith, better knowledge
and affection. That is what keeps me awake, that difficult
hope.

My hope, I must say, subsists on an extremely meager
diet—a reducer's diet. It takes some strength from the
knowledge that we may be looking doom squarely in the face,
from the knowledge that human beings, let alone human so-
cieties, cannot live indefinitely by poison and fire. It takes
some strength from knowing that more and more people
seem to have this knowledge; more and more people seem to
know that we now have to choose consciously, perhaps for
the first time in human history, between doom and something better.

My hope feeds, however uneasily, on such a phrase as "the
forest commons" that has recently floated up into public dis-
cussion. I think I know the worry and the hope from which
that phrase comes. It comes from a growing awareness of the
mutuality of the health of human beings and the health of na-

ture, and this is encouraging. I am uneasy about it because I think I know also what the word "commons" means. It means a property belonging to a community, which the community members are free to use because they will use it with culturally prescribed care and restraint. I do not think that this even remotely applies to us.

Historically, the commons belonged to the *local* community, not to "the public." The possibility of a commons, in the true sense, depends on local adaptation, a process in which Americans have, at times and in places, made a few credible beginnings, always frustrated by the still-dominant belief that local adaptation does not matter because localities do not matter. At present it is generally true that we do not know in any useful sense where we are, much less how to act on the basis of such knowledge. If we humans know where we are and how to live well and conservingly there, then we can have and use the place "in common." Otherwise—and it is still far otherwise with us—we must find appropriate ways to parcel out, and so limit, both privilege and responsibility.

The idea of a commons applies perhaps to most tribal cultures. It applied to English culture before the long and bitter history of enclosure. It applied, for a while, in New England. But we in Kentucky, as in most of the rest of the United States, never had such an idea. We have had the idea of private property, the idea of public property, and the idea of the commonwealth—and we have valued those ideas in about that order. We have never thought very well or very thoroughly about any of those ideas. Nevertheless, I prefer the word "commonwealth" (in its literal and now somewhat outdated sense) to the word "commons," for the very reason that "commonwealth" comes to us with so great a historical burden. We have been saying it and ignoring it for so long that though it accurately names our condition and our hope, it is not likely to lead to too much optimism. Too much optimism, I am afraid, will lead us to understand by "commons" only what we have so far understood by "public"—and that clearly would solve none of our problems.

In my own politics and economics I am a Jeffersonian—or, I might more accurately say, I am a democrat and an agrarian. I believe that land that is to be used should be divided into small parcels among a lot of small owners; I believe therefore in the right of private property. I believe that, given our history and tradition, a large population of small property holders offers the best available chance for local cultural adaptation and good stewardship of the land—provided that the property holders are secure, legally and economically, in their properties.

To say that the right of private property has often been used to protect individuals and even global corporations in their greed is not to say that it cannot secure individuals in an appropriate economic share in their country and in a consequent economic and political independence, just as Thomas Jefferson thought it could. That is the political justification of the right of private property. There is also, I believe, an ecological justification. If landed properties are democratically divided and properly scaled, and if family security in these properties can be preserved over a number of generations, then we will greatly increase the possibility of authentic cultural adaptation to local homelands. Not only will we make more apparent to successive generations the necessary identity between the health of human communities and the health of local ecosystems but we will also give people the best motives for caretaking and we will call into service the necessary local intelligence and imagination. Such an arrangement would give us the fullest possible assurance that our forests and farmlands would be used by people who know them best and care the most about them.

My interest here is in preserving the possibility of intimacy in the use of the land. Some of us still understand the elaborate care necessary to preserve marital and familial and social intimacy, but I am arguing also for the necessity of preserving silvicultural and agricultural intimacy. The possibility of intimacy between worker and place is virtually identical with the possibility of good work. True intimacy in work, as in love, means lifelong commitment; it means knowing what you are doing. The industrial consumer and the industrial producer believe that after any encounter between people or between people and the world there will be no consequences. The consumptive society is interested in sterile or inconsequential intimacy, which is a fantasy. But suppose, on the contrary, that we try to serve the cultural forms and imperatives that prepare adequately for the convergence of need with fertility, of human life with the natural world. *Then* we must think of consequences; we must think of the children.

I am an uneasy believer in the right of private property because I know that this right can be understood as the right to destroy property, which is to say the natural or the given world. I do not believe that such a right exists, even though its presumed existence has covered the destruction of a lot of land. A considerable amount of this destruction has been allowed by our granting to corporations the status of "persons" capable of holding "private property." Most corporate abuse or destruction of land must be classified, I think, as either willing or intentional. The willingness to use land on a large scale implies inevitably at least a willingness to damage it. But because we have had, alongside our history of land abuse, a tradition or at least a persistent hope of agrarian economy and settled community life, the damage to the land that has been done by individual owners is more likely to be attributable to ignorance or to economic constraint. To speak sensibly of property and of the rights and uses of property, we must always observe this fundamental distinction between corporate property and property that is truly private—that is, property of modest or appropriate size owned by an individual.

Our history, obviously, gives us no hope that, in our present lack of a general culture of land stewardship, the weaknesses in our idea of private property can be corrected by the idea of public property.

There is some hope, I think, in the idea of the commonwealth, which seems to acknowledge that we all have a common interest or share in the land, an interest that precedes our interest in private property. Of the precedence of our share in the common wealth the best evidence is that we share also a common health; the two, in fact, are inseparable. If we have the "right to life," as we have always supposed, then that right must stand upon the further right to air, water, food, clothing, and shelter.

It follows that every person exercising the right to hold private property has an obligation to secure to the rest of us the right to live from that property. He or she has an obligation to use it in such a way as to not impair or diminish our rightful interest in it.

But—and here is the catch—that obligation on the part of the landowner implies a concurrent obligation on the part of society as a whole. If we give our proxy to the landowner to use—and, as is always implied, to take care of—the land on our behalf, then we are obliged to make the landowner able to afford not only to use the land but also to care properly for it. This is where the grossest error of our civilization shows itself.

In giving a few farmers our proxies to produce food in the public behalf for very little economic return, we have also given them our proxies to care for the land in the public behalf for no economic return at all. This is our so-called cheap-food policy, which is in fact an antifarming policy, an antifarmer policy, and an antiland policy. We have also a cheap-timber policy, which is similarly calamitous.

We hold the land under a doctrine of private property that in practice acknowledges no commonwealth. By allowing or forcing the owners and users of productive land to share in the commonwealth so minimally that they are poorly paid for their work and not paid at all for their stewardship, we have stood an ancient pyramid on its tip. We now have an enormous population of urban consumers dependent on a tiny population of rural producers. And this involves a number of problems that are not merely quantitative or practical.

In her paper "Agricultural Industrialization and the Loss of Biodiversity," my friend Laura Jackson helps us to see that as farming families dwindle away, we lose not just essential and perhaps irreplaceable knowledge but also an old appreciation and affection that may be even more valuable. Here is what she says about the industrialization of livestock production; though she is talking about agriculture, her principle applies just as obviously to forestry:

> While innovative farmers can still raise hogs and dairy cattle more cheaply and with fewer environmental impacts than the high-density livestock facility, they suffer as their neighbors go out of business and the infrastructure and markets for livestock crumble. . . . Without a market to sell their animals, even the most practical, conscientious, and sustainable operations, including those of the Amish and Mennonites, are in danger of disappearing. When the minds responsible for these farms have left the countryside, replaced by minimum-wage labor in factory-style facilities, so will the potential to conserve and improve the agricultural landscape.

Conservationists have now begun to acknowledge that the health and productivity of the land constitute a commonwealth. I say they have *begun* to acknowledge this because at present they tend to acknowledge it only so far as it pertains to forested or otherwise "wild" land, the land that most conservationists understand as "natural." They wish to protect the common wealth of the forested land by some such doctrine as "the forest commons." But the danger is that this will accomplish only one more anomalous inversion; from a doctrine of private landownership that acknowledges no commonwealth, we might go to a doctrine of commonwealth in which there are no private shares. "The forest commons," I am afraid, may become an idea that will separate forestry and forest conservation from the rural economy, just as industrial agriculture is an idea that has separated farming and soil conservation from the rural economy.

To insist that our public forests should be cared for and used as a commonwealth already strains belief, for it raises immediately the question of where we are to find the people who know how and are adequately motivated to care for it. Our history—which is still the history of a colonial economy—could not produce an adequate number of people adequately prepared to be good stewards of the public lands any more than of lands "privately" owned. Colonial economies place no value on stewardship, and do not teach, encourage, reward, or even protect it.

To remedy this failure, we will have to realize that not just forest land but *all* land, private and public, farmed or forested, is "natural." All land is natural and all nature is a common wealth. Wherever we live, we live in nature and by using nature, and this use everywhere implies the requirement of good stewardship. But we will have to do more than merely change our minds. We will have to implement a different kind of education and a different kind of economy.

If in order to protect our forest land we designate it a commons or commonwealth separate from private ownership, then who will care for it? The absentee timber companies who see no reason to care about local consequences? The same government agencies and agents who are failing at present to take good care of our public forests? Is it credible that people inadequately skilled and inadequately motivated to care well for the land can be *made* to care well for it by public insistence that they do so?

The answer is obvious: you cannot get good care in the use of the land by demanding it from public officials. That you have the legal right to demand it does not at all improve the case. If one out of every two of us should become a public official, we would be no nearer to good land stewardship than we are now. The idea that a displaced people might take appropriate care of places is merely absurd; there is no sense in it and no hope. Our present ideas of conservation and of public stewardship are not enough. Duty is not enough. Sentiment is not enough. No mere law, divine or human, could conceivably be enough to protect the land while we are using it.

If we want the land to be cared for, then we must have people living on and from the land who are able and willing to care for it. If   as the idea of commonwealth clearly implies—landowners and land users are accountable to their fellow citizens for their work, their products, and their stewardship, then these landowners and land users must be granted an equitable membership in the economy.

Thirty years ago, one of the organizations leading the fight against strip mining was the Appalachian Group to Save the Land and the People. This seemed an exemplary organization—an informed local response to a local calamity—and I was strongly affected and influenced by it. What most impressed me was the complexity of purpose announced in its name: it proposed to save the land *and* the people. This seems to me still an inescapable necessity. You really cannot specialize the work of conservation. You cannot save the land apart from the people or the people apart from the land. To save either, you must save both—that is a lesson taught nowhere better than in the economic history of the Commonwealth of Kentucky. To save both the land and the people, you need a strong rural economy. In truth, you need several strong rural economies, for even so small a state as ours has many regions, and a good economy joins local people conservingly to their local landscapes.

If we are serious about conservation, then we are going to have to quit thinking of our work as a sequence of specialized and temporary responses to a sequence of specialized and temporary emergencies. We will have to realize finally that our work is economic. We are going to have to come up with competent, practical, at-home answers to the humblest human questions: How should we live? How should we keep house? How should we provide ourselves with food, clothing, shelter, heat, light, learning, amusement, rest? How, in short, ought we to use the world?

No conservation issue could lead more directly to those questions than the issue of Kentucky forestry. It is true that our state contains some sizable areas of private or public forest land, but we cannot proceed on the assumption that we are dealing with large tracts of timber or that we can ever hope to conserve our forests solely by forest conservation policies, however enlightened.

In Kentucky we have 12,700,000 acres of forest, more than 90 percent of which is privately owned. We must assume, I think, that many of the 440,000 owners of this land would fiercely oppose any public appropriation of their modest properties or any diminution of their rights therein. Although I know very well the dangers to the common wealth and health inherent in private property rights, I would be one of those fierce opposers.

The first of my reasons is my too little faith in the long-term efficacy of public stewardship. Perhaps the public will prove equal to the task of wilderness preservation, though that is by no means certain. But it's not easy to imagine the conditions under which highly competent and responsible public stewardship of land that is in use might be maintained for many generations and through the inevitable changes of politics and economics.

My second reason is that I do have some faith in the long-term efficacy of private stewardship, again provided that the connection between the people and the land can be made secure. To be preserved in use, even our public lands must come to be intimately connected to their local communities by means of strong local economies.

The two great ruiners of privately owned land, as I have said, are ignorance and economic constraint. And these tend to be related. People have ruined land mainly by overusing it—by forcing it to produce beyond its power to recover or by forcing it to produce what it never should have been asked to produce. And behind this overuse, almost always, has been economic need. Sometimes ignorance and poverty have been directly related: the land would have produced better immediately had it been better used. But economic constraint also preserves ignorance in land use: families have often failed or starved out before they had time to learn to use the land well. Land that passes rapidly from one owner or user to another will not be adequately studied or learned and so will almost predictably be abused. The more marginal or difficult the land, the worse will be the abuse.

This work of ignorance and economic constraint, moreover, has been abetted by our time's radical and artificial division of the producer's interest in the land from the interest of the consumer. In reality, these two interests are the same, and yet our idea of "the market" has encouraged us to think of the interests of producer and consumer as two interests, not only divided but competitive. And we have allowed many economic enterprises and many agencies to interpose themselves between producers and consumers, greatly increasing our bewilderment about our economy, our connection to the land and to one another, and our ecological and economic responsibilities. One result, to name only the most prominent, is our so-called cheap-food policy, by which farmers are put under pressure to abuse the land on behalf of urban consumers, many of whom think of themselves as conservationists.

In Kentucky we are now moving rapidly toward the end of such economic fantasy. Conservationists wishing to establish good forestry practices in our state will immediately see the hopelessness of conventional economics and of conventional conservation if only they will consider that many of the owners of Kentucky's forests are farmers, and therefore that one of the greatest threats to our forests is the continuing stress within our agricultural economy. We would-be conservers of the state's forests must see that the interests of producers and consumers, of landowners and conservationists are not divided but only the two sides of a mutuality of interest that waits to be defined. Conservation clearly cannot advance much farther here unless conservationists can make common cause with small landowners and land users. And our state's small farmers and other small landowners desperately need the understanding and help of conservationists.

I would beg my fellow conservationists, as I would beg my fellow farmers, to realize that we must quit thinking of our countryside piecemeal, in terms of separate products or enterprises: tobacco, timber, livestock, vegetables, feed grains, recreation, and so on. We must begin to think of the human use of each of our regions or localities as one economy, both rural and urban, involving all the local products. We must learn to see such local economies as the best and perhaps the only means we have of preserving that system of ecological and cultural connections that is, inescapably, our common wealth.

If conservationists are serious about conservation, they will have to realize that the best conserver of land in use will always be the small owner or operator, farmer or forester or both, who lives within a securely placed family and community, who knows how to use the land in the best way, and who can afford to do so. Conservationists who are also farmers or foresters already feel the tension between the demands of ecology and the demands of our present economy; they already feel the urgency of our need for a better economy and better work.

Now consumer-conservationists must begin to feel these strains and stresses also. They will have to acquaint themselves with the requirements of good agriculture. They will have to see that a good food economy does not enrich the agribusiness and grocery corporations at the expense of everything and everybody else, but pays to the real producers the real costs of good food production in capital, labor, skill, and care. They will have to become active and knowledgeable participants in their local food economies. They will have to see that their local Sierra Club chapter is no more important to conservation than their local food-marketing co-op.

Similarly, they will have to understand the value of and give their support and patronage to the formation of good local forest economies, permanently in place, scaled so as to use the local forests in the best way, and able to pay a price for timber that will encourage the best forestry and logging practices. These three issues of local economy, scale, and price will determine the quality of use. Our present economy pretty well dictates that a farmer's woodlot or forested hillside will be roughly logged once in a generation or once in a lifetime, and otherwise ignored or used for grazing. A good local forest economy would both protect the forest from abuse and make it a continuing source of income to the landowner and the local community.

Let me give just one very suggestive example of what I mean. My friend Gene Logsdon owns fourteen acres of woodland in Ohio, and his son, Jerry, has a small woodworking shop. One of Gene's main reasons for owning his wooded acreage is that he likes trees. He likes to walk in his woods and look at the wildflowers or watch warblers in the spring. His two woodlots would be valueless or even repugnant to him as fourteen acres of stumps. At the same time, a part of his fascination with his small farm, including his woodlots, is in his economic relation to it. He uses his land because using it makes economic sense and gives pleasure. He logs his woodlands very selectively for firewood and lumber, taking mostly dead or dying or defective trees—and always leaving some dead trees in hospitality to the birds and animals. Every few years he accumulates enough logs for a day's sawing, and then he hires a man with a portable band saw to come and saw the logs into boards. Here is what he wrote to me in response to something I had written about local forest economies:

> You could have made the point that not only do woodlot owners lack bargaining power but when the wood comes back to the local lumberyard the price is atrocious. Jerry tells me that the last time we had the band saw man in to saw logs, we came away from a day's work with something like 3,000 board feet of good white oak lumber, worth $3,000 or $4,000, and this was all from blemished or poor-grade logs that we could not have sold at all to a timber buyer. The band sawyer charged us $350! Not only that, but we got a few board feet of mulberry, pear, and sassafras for furniture accents. The mulberry and pear were

big old yard trees that a regular sawmill would never take because of possible hardware in the log. A band sawyer can take the risk of hitting a nail because a dulled band-saw blade can be sharpened for $15.

This is an excellent example of intimacy in land use. This is the way a good forest economy reaches the ground. Such intimacy enables pleasure, good care, attention to details, awareness of small opportunities, diversity, and thrift. It prevents abuse, preserves the forest, and produces an economic return. A fourteen-acre woodland that supplies a household's winter heat and $1,000 worth of sawed lumber a year is contributing significant income—considerably more, in fact, than an equal acreage of corn. We should note in passing that Gene's woodlands have produced this income probably without diminishment of their value as standing timber. Moreover, as he well knows, such farm woodlands might also produce fence posts, medicinal or edible herbs, Christmas wreaths, mushrooms, and other products usable or marketable. We must also understand that this sort of forestry and forest economics cannot expectably or even imaginably be practiced by a public agency or a timber company.

But let us not limit our thinking just to the economics of woodlands. Let us think of the thousands of farm woodlands in Kentucky not just as the possible basis of a system of good regional forest economies but as parts of family farms that include, in addition to their woodlands, some land that is arable and some that is in permanent pasture. Such farms in Kentucky are capable of producing an astonishing variety of marketable products: forest products, livestock, row crops, herbs and mushrooms, fruits and vegetables. They can produce these good and necessary things in great abundance indefinitely, protecting in the process the commonwealth of air, water, forests, and soils, granted only the one condition: vigorous local economies capable of supporting a stable and capable rural population, rewarding them appropriately for both their products and their stewardship. The development of such economies ought to be the primary aim of our conservation effort. Such development is not only desirable; it is increasingly necessary and increasingly urgent.

The Conservation
of Nature and
the Preservation
of Humanity

In the fall of 1993 the production in Washington, D.C., and on Broadway of *The Kentucky Cycle*, by Robert Schenkkan, called forth an unprecedented outcry of objection from eastern Kentucky, which was the setting for Mr. Schenkkan's cycle of plays. The substance of the protest was that Mr. Schenkkan, like too many before him, had presented Kentucky mountaineers (with a few politically correct exceptions) as ignorant, vicious hillbillies who, in their thoughtless violence and greed, had made for themselves exactly the fate that they deserved.

Perhaps the best clue to the nature of this controversy lies in a long article about Mr. Schenkkan and *The Kentucky Cycle* that Ross Wetzsteon published in *The Village Voice* on November 9, 1993. Mr. Wetzsteon quotes Mr. Schenkkan as saying that "what I'm trying to do in *The Kentucky Cycle* is show how and why the myths that once sustained us now fail us." The failure of these myths, which are the frontier myths of abundance and escape, has caused what Mr. Schenkkan calls "dissociation"—"the lack of connection between people, the lack of connection between people and the land." And he says that "we need myths of preservation and responsibility," which he apparently believes now need to be invented.

At the heart of the Kentuckians' argument against *The Kentucky Cycle* is Mr. Schenkkan's failure to see that this second set of "myths" is already alive in eastern Kentucky. There as elsewhere—but probably more there than in most places—they are subordinate myths, for during most of this century, the dominant history in the region has been that of the exploitation of timber and coal and people. But the contrary impulse of preservation and responsibility has survived. It has survived in hundreds of dooryards, kitchen gardens, and small farms in valleys where the coal companies have never come. It has survived in numerous local individuals and groups whose purpose has been, as one of them put it, "to save the land and the people." It has survived in the writings of Harry Caudill, James Still, Harriet Arnow, Gurney Norman, and others. It has survived in an indomitable local

newspaper, *The Mountain Eagle*. It has survived in local institutions like Appalshop and Appalachia–Science in the Public
Interest. Local people, some of them heroes, have opposed
strip mining from the moment it began. All of this Mr.
Schenkkan, who spent only one day in eastern Kentucky,
failed to understand.

The point, as I see it, is that if we want to oppose the forces
of social and ecological irresponsibility, we do not need "new
myths" invented by writers and intellectuals, for in the myth
department—if we are going to use Mr. Schenkkan's term—
we already have what we need. As Harlan Hubbard once said,
"what we need is at hand." The myth of preservation and responsibility exists, and some people—though by no means
enough—have understood its implications.

The case of *The Kentucky Cycle*, which won a Pulitzer Prize,
is of more than local interest because Mr. Schenkkan's plays
are representative of a sort of one-eyed, politically correct
criticism of American history and of Western cultural tradition that is a danger both to understanding and to the possibility of improvement. Mr. Schenkkan is at fault in his play
and what he has said about it not because his history is
wrong, for he is right about our inheritance of greed and destruction, but because it is incomplete. It has become too
easy to suppose that American history has been entirely
determined by the experience of the frontier, and moreover that our frontier experience was determined entirely
by arrogance, violence, and greed. Even the history of the
frontier is more complex than that. When history has been

reduced to cliché, we need to return to the study of history.

I considered it a privilege to be able to turn from my thoughts about Robert Schenkkan and the Kentucky mountains to thoughts about Wallace Stegner and the American West. For Wallace Stegner was not only the more complete historian by far, but often as a historian he had the authority of an autobiographer. He lived through, saw with his own eyes, and knew intimately much of the history that he wrote about.

We certainly have had no better student of the workings of our frontier irresponsibility. Wallace Stegner was born into the failed and still-failing frontier dream of easy wealth and easy escape—the dream of the people he called "boomers"—that motivated both the westward movement of the frontier and the industrialization that followed. He recognized the powerful influence of this myth in his father, who "wanted to make a killing and end up on Easy Street" but who was driven, first by hope and then by failure, from one money-making scheme to another, and finally to ruin. This, in American boomers, was actually less a myth than a mental condition that Stegner described as "exaggerated, uninformed, unrealistic, greedy expectation." In his own early experience, this expectation led to the plowing of the prairie in southwestern Saskatchewan—prairie that was "totally unsuited to be plowed up." The same expectation led to the settlement of the American West on the basis not of sound local knowledge but of presumption and pipe dream. Of *The Big Rock Candy Mountain*, Stegner wrote, "I had been trying to paint a portrait of my father"—not realizing until later that "my father was also a type." But even in that early novel, there is evidence that he already recognized the type as such and accurately understood its bias:

> Why remain in one dull plot of earth when Heaven was reachable, was touchable, was just over there? The whole race was like the fir tree in the fairy tale which wanted to be cut down and dressed up with lights and bangles and colored paper, and see the world and be a Christmas tree.

In his later books, Stegner gives much attention and no little grief to the results, human and natural, of the "feeding frenzy" that inevitably accompanied the entrance of an uninformed and limitless greed into a land that was both abundant and fragile.

But unlike many recent commentators on our history, Stegner knew also that as a people, we were not conditioned entirely by the inordinate desires and acts of the boomers. There was, virtually from the beginning, a countertheme, the theme of settlement, which always implied the "myths of preservation and responsibility" that Mr. Schenkkan talks about. Stegner was born into this theme also; he knew it in his mother, of whom he wrote in *The Big Rock Candy Mountain*:

> She wanted to be part of something, an essential atom in a street, a town, a state; she would have loved to get herself expressed in all the pleasant, secure details of a deeply lived-in house.

Later, I think, he realized that his mother, in this sense, was also a type. Not all who came to American places came to plunder and run. Some came to stay, or came with the hope of staying. These Stegner called "stickers" or "nesters." They were moved by an articulate hope, already ancient by the time of Columbus, of a settled, independent, frugal life on a small freehold. We can find this hope in Hesiod, in the fourth of Virgil's *Georgics*, in the 128th Psalm. This was the vision that we finally came to call "Jeffersonian"—a free nation of authentically and securely landed people. Stegner knew that this vision, though it may have been a secondary influence on our history, was nevertheless a considerable one. He knew that it could not be left out of account. His preference for settlement, I think, explains his sustained and respectful interest in the Mormons. Of himself he said, "I was at heart a nester, like my mother."

Thus, it is possible—and probably necessary—to think of Wallace Stegner's work as taking form within the tensions between these historical opposites: boomer and sticker, exploitation and settlement, caring and not caring, life adapted to available technology and personal desire and life adapted to a known place. But to lay out these pairs of opposites is not simply to define a moral choice, though it certainly is to do that; it is also to define a historical and cultural split that characterizes us as Americans. And by "us" I mean all of us. I don't think this characterization can be successfully limited to any group—political, racial, sexual, or otherwise. All of us, I think, are in some manner torn between caring and not caring, staying and going.

Wallace Stegner obviously made the correct moral choice —that is, he chose to be like his mother and not like his father—but not in the sense that he ever finished making it. Having chosen one way, one is never free of the opposite way. A good deal of the power in Stegner's work, for example, comes from his thorough understanding of his father, an understanding that involved sympathy—that involved undoubtedly the recognition of himself in his father and of his father in himself. Such choices are not clean-cut and final, as when we choose one of two forks in a road, but they involve us in tension, in tendency. We must keep on choosing.

If enough of us were to choose caring over not caring, staying over going, then the culture would change, the theme of exploitation would become subordinate to the theme of settlement, and then the choice to be a sticker would become easier. The necessary examples would be more numerous and more available. The way would be clearer.

As we know, we are under increasing pressure to choose caring over not caring. We know that caring will involve us in great effort and discomfort, and we dread to choose it, but we know too that the toils and miseries of not caring are becoming greater by the day. Someday, presumably, it will become easier and less miserable to care than not to care—if by then we still remember how to care, and if the choice is still possible.

Many of us, in fact, already have a conscious preference for caring. Some of us, perhaps, have been stickers all along: maybe we were born into the underclass of settlers. Anyhow, we have taken the side of care. We know that we need to live in a world that is cared for. The ubiquitous clichés about saving the planet and walking lightly on the earth testify to this.

But I believe that all of us who prefer caring over not caring are going to have to study very closely the implications of our preference. For we not only need to think beyond our own clichés; we also need to make sure that we don't carry over into our efforts at conservation and preservation the moral assumptions and habits of thought of the culture of exploitation. So far, it seems to me, we have done just that: we have incorporated in our efforts to preserve the natural health and wealth of the world a number of the assumptions that have made such an effort necessary.

The most persistent and the most dangerous of these is the assumption that some parts of the world can be preserved while others are abused or destroyed. As necessary as it obviously is, the effort of "wilderness preservation" has too often implied that it is enough to save a series of islands of pristine and uninhabited wilderness in an otherwise exploited, damaged, and polluted land. And, further, that the pristine wilderness is the only alternative to exploitation and abuse. So far, the moral landscape of the conservation movement has tended to be a landscape of extremes, which you can see pictured in any number of expensive books of what I suppose must be called "conservation photography." On the one hand we have the unspoiled wilderness, and on the other hand we have scenes of utter devastation—strip mines, clearcuts, industrially polluted wastelands, and so on. We wish, say the conservationists, to have more of the one and less of the other. To which, of course, one must say amen. But it must be a qualified amen, for the conservationists' program is embarrassingly incomplete. Its picture of the world as either deserted landscape or desertified landscape is too simple; it misrepresents both the world and humanity. If we are to have an accurate picture of the world, even in its present diseased condition, we must interpose between the unused landscape and the misused landscape a landscape that humans have used well.

That there have been and are well-used landscapes we know, and to leave these landscapes out of account is to leave out humanity at its best. It is certainly necessary to keep in mind the image of the human being as parasite and wrecker—what e. e. cummings called "this busy monster manunkind"—for it is dangerous not to know this possibility in ourselves. And certainly we must preserve some places unchanged; there should be places, and times too, in which we do nothing. But we must also include ourselves as makers, as economic creatures with livings to make, who have the ability, if we will use it, to work in ways that are stewardly and kind toward all that we must use. That is, we must include ourselves as human beings in the fullest sense of the term, understanding ourselves in the fullness of our cultural inheritance and our legitimate hopes.

We must include ourselves because whether we choose to do so or not, we are included. We who are now alive are living in this world; we are not dead, nor do we have another world to live in. There are, then, two laws that we had better take to be absolute.

The first is that as we cannot exempt ourselves from living in this world, then if we wish to live, we cannot exempt ourselves from using the world. Even the most scrupulous vegetarians must use the world—that is, they must kill creatures, substitute one species for another, and eat food that otherwise would be eaten by other creatures. And so by the standard of absolute harmlessness, the two available parties are not vegetarians and meat eaters but rather eaters and noneaters. Us eaters have got 'em greatly outnumbered.

If we cannot exempt ourselves from use, then we must deal with the issues raised by use. And so the second law is that if we want to continue living, we cannot exempt use from care.

A third law (perhaps not absolute, but virtually so) is that if we want to use the world with care, we cannot exempt ourselves from our cultural inheritance, our tradition. This is a delicate subject at present because our cultural tradition happens to be Western, and there is now a fashion of disfavor toward the Western tradition. But most of us are in the Western tradition somewhat as we are in the world: we are in it because we were born in it. We can't get out of it because it made us what we are; we are, to some extent, what it is. And perhaps we would not like to get out of it if that meant giving up, as we would have to do, our language and its literature, our hereditary belief that all people matter individually, our heritage of democracy, liberty, civic responsibility, stewardship, and so on. This tradition obviously involves errors and mistakes, damages and tragedies. But that only means that the tradition too must be used with care. It is properly subject to critical intelligence and is just as properly subject to helps and influences from other traditions. But criticize and qualify it as we may, we cannot get along without it, for we have no other way to learn care; and in fact care is a subject about which our tradition has much to teach.

And so I am proposing that in order to preserve the health of nature, we must preserve ourselves as human beings—as creatures who possess humanity not just as a collection of physical attributes but also as the cultural imperative to be caretakers, good neighbors to one another and to the other creatures.

Whether we consider it from a religious point of view or from the point of view of our merely practical wish to continue to live, our presence in this varied and fertile world is our perpetual crisis. It forces upon us constantly a virtual curriculum of urgent questions: Can we adapt our work and our pleasure to our places so as to live in them without destroying them? That is, can we make adequately practical and pleasing local cultures? Are we Americans capable of an authentic (which is to say a land-based) multiculturalism? Can we limit our work and our economies to a scale appropriate to our places, to our place in the order of things, and to our intelligence? Can we understand ourselves as creatures of limited and modest intelligence? Can we control ourselves? Can we get beyond the assumption that it is possible to live inhumanely and yet "save the planet" by a series of last-minute preservations of things perceived at the last minute to be endangered and, only because endangered, precious?

When we include ourselves as parts or belongings of the world we are trying to preserve, then obviously we can no longer think of the world as "the environment"—something out there around us. We can see that our relation to the world surpasses mere connection and verges on identity. And we can see that our right to live in this world, whose parts we are, is a right that is strictly conditioned. We come face to face with the law I mentioned a while ago: If we want to become "stickers," even if we merely want to live, we cannot exempt use from care. There is simply nothing in Creation that does not matter. Our tradition instructs us that this is so, and it is being proved to be so, every day, by our experience. We cannot be improved—in fact, we cannot help but be damaged—by our useless or greedy or merely ignorant destruction of anything.

Once we have understood that we cannot exempt from our care anything at all that we have the power to damage—which now means everything in the world—then we face yet another startling realization: we have reclaimed and revalidated the ground of our moral and religious tradition. We now can see that what we have traditionally called "sins" are wrong not because they are forbidden but because they divide us from our neighbors, from the world, and ultimately from God. They deny care and are dangerous to creatures.

As an example, I would offer Philip Sherrard's definition of avarice in his invaluable book *Human Image: World Image*. Avarice, he says,

> is a disposition of our soul which refuses to acknowledge and share in the destiny common to all things and which desires to possess and use all things for itself. . . . Through this seeming act of self-aggrandizement we actually debase

the whole of our existence, perverting and even destroying the natural harmony of our being as well as that of everything with which we come into contact.

Avarice, then, is a sin for very practical reasons: it makes division within unity, disorder within order, and discord within harmony. This is exactly Ezra Pound's understanding of the related sin of vanity—and here again the appeal is to harmony with the natural or created order:

> Pull down thy vanity, it is not man
> Made courage, or made order, or made grace,
>   Pull down thy vanity, I say pull down.
> Learn of the green world what can be thy place
> In scaled invention or true artistry.

Pound was not always sane, but in those lines he is sane as few modern people have been.

What we have traditionally called "virtues," on the other hand, are good not because they have been highly recommended but because they are necessary; they make for unity and harmony. Faith, to speak only of the highest of the traditional virtues, is our life's instinctive leap toward its origin, the motion by which we acknowledge the order and harmony to which we belong. To deny that this is so is not to destroy faith but only to reduce and misdirect it, for faith of some kind is apparently necessary also in the sense that we cannot escape it; we have to have some version of it. Our instinct for faith is like a well-bred Border collie, who, lacking cattle or sheep, will herd children or chickens or cats. If we don't direct our faith toward God or into some authentic "way" of the soul, then we direct it toward progress or science or weaponry or education or nature or human nature or doctors or gurus or genetic engineers or computers or NASA. And as we reduce the objects of our faith and so reduce our faith, we inevitably reduce ourselves. We are by nature creatures of faith, as perhaps all creatures are; we all live by counting on things that cannot be proved. As creatures of faith, we must choose either to be religious or to be superstitious, to believe in things that cannot be proved or to believe in things that can be disproved. The present age is an age of superstition, and some of our shallowest superstitions have the authorization of our hardest-headed rationalists and realists. The modern ambition to control nature, for instance, is an ambition based foursquare on a superstition: the idea that what we take nature to be is what nature is, or that nature is that to which it can be reduced. If nature is to be controlled, then it has to be reduced to that which is theoretically controllable. It must be understood as a machine or as the sum of its known, separable, and decipherable parts.

Care, on the contrary, rests upon genuine religion. Care allows creatures to escape our explanations into their actual presence and their essential mystery. In taking care of fellow creatures, we acknowledge that they are not ours; we acknowledge that they belong to an order and a harmony of which we ourselves are parts. To answer to the perpetual crisis of our presence in this abounding and dangerous world, we have only the perpetual obligation of care.

The idea that we cannot exempt anything from care is of course difficult, because it is difficult to care for all things. As creatures of modest intelligence, we ought perhaps to fear that it is impossible. And yet it is this very difficulty that is the key to our place and role as human beings. To be fully human, we must accept the likelihood that several or even many things may at the same time be of ultimate importance. This should at least save us from the folly of trying to solve "environmental" problems one at a time. It should inform us that we are dealing with the issue of health in its largest and also its most literal sense: creaturely orders and communities that are whole. And so we see that we must be whole ourselves, for the good solutions must come from our wholeness, our affection and reverence, not from our sense of duty, much less from desperation.

We have tried on a large scale the experiment of preferring ourselves to the exclusion of all other creatures, with results that are manifestly disastrous. And now, conscious of those results, we are tempted to correct them by denigrating ourselves, by wishing somehow to efface ourselves. But that is only the opposite kind of self-indulgence, utterly worthless as an answer to any problem. Misanthropy is not the remedy for "anthropocentrism." Finally we must see that we cannot be made kind toward our fellow creatures except by the same qualities that make us kind toward our fellow humans.

The problem obviously is that we are not well practiced in kindness toward our fellow humans. In the course of our unprecedented inhumanity toward other creatures and the world, we have become unprecedentedly inhumane toward humans—and especially, I think, toward human children.

I know of nothing that so strongly calls into question our ability to care for the world as our present abuses of our own reproductivity. How can we take care of other creatures, all born like ourselves from the world's miraculous fecundity, if we have forsaken the qualities of culture and character that inform the nurture of children?

Maybe it is because our society is so dominated by the economic ideal of productivity that we have no time for young people (and old people), who are not highly productive. Or maybe it is because of our rather frivolous idea of personal freedom that we shrug off the claims of those most in need and most deserving of our care. Or maybe it is the fault of an economy that now requires both parents of many families to work away from home. Or maybe it is the increasing commercialization of family relationships, according to which nobody, not even a husband or a wife, should do anything for anybody else that is not compensated by a price agreed upon in advance.

Whatever the reason, it is a fact that we are now conducting a sort of general warfare against children, who are being aborted or abandoned, abused, drugged, bombed, neglected, poorly raised, poorly fed, poorly taught, and poorly disciplined. Many of them will not only find no worthy work but no work of any kind. All of them will inherit a diminished, diseased, and poisoned world. We will visit upon them not only our sins but also our debts. We have set before them thousands of examples—governmental, industrial, and recreational—suggesting that the violent way is the best way. And then we have the hypocrisy to be surprised and troubled when they carry guns and use them. Our mistreatment of children is not mitigated by our interest in "reforming" the institutions into which we put them. We will not have better children by having better day care centers, schools, and jails.

There are of course many parents who care properly for their children, and the traditions of good upbringing still survive. But like the traditions of good land use, these traditions of family life have become subordinate, and they are having a hard time. As a lot of parents have found out, it is not easy to bring up your children in a way that is significantly different from the way your neighbors are bringing up their children.

A child psychologist told me not long ago that he frequently sees four-year-olds who when asked "Who loves you?" reply, "I don't know." If we have even a suspicion that we must not exempt anything from care, how can we bear this? And yet this neglect is hedged around on every side by talk of rights and freedoms and careers and professions.

Abortion, for instance, which might be defensible as a tragic choice acceptable in the most straitened circumstances, is defended as a "right" derived from "the right of a woman to control her own body." The right of any person to control her or his own body, subject to the usual qualifications, is incontestable—or, at any rate, it is not going to be contested by me. But the usual qualifications hold that if you can control your own body only by destroying another person's body, then control has come much too late. Self-mastery is the appropriate way to control one's own body, not surgery.

I am well aware of the argument that a fetus is not a child until it can live outside the womb, but I am aware also that every creature is surrounded by such questions of dependency and viability all its life. If we are unworthy to live as long as we are dependent on life-supporting conditions, then none of us has any rights. And I would not try to convince any farmer or gardener that the planted seed newly sprouted is not a crop.

Let us suppose on the contrary, as we once did suppose, as some of us still do, that it is the right of every child, from conception, to have the care of both parents—would that not go far toward growing us up out of our present sexual childishness and delusion?

As we humans come of age and enter into sexuality, we surely confront yet another law that we had better understand: sex and fertility are joined. We have spent a lot of effort and money to disjoin them, and have generated a lot of giddy propaganda about our supposed success—but we have also a lot of evidence to prove our failure, and I mean the numbers of childhood pregnancies, single parents, abortions, abandoned babies, babies kept but unwanted, children raised by public institutions and TV.

How is it that we come to these issues of sexuality in worrying about the conservation of nature? Well, for a reason that ought to be obvious: if sex and fertility are joined, then sex and the world are joined. Sex is a part of the world's wilderness; it is a part of our wildness. To say that we must be careful of it is not to say that we must make it tame but rather that we must not damage it or ourselves by ignorance or foolishness. The world's wilderness, wherever we meet it, requires

us, at a minimum, to grow up, to rid ourselves of false assumptions about who and where we are. To grow up is to go
beyond our inborn selfishness and arrogance; to be grown up
is to know that the self is not a place to live.

It is wrong to assume that sex carries us into a personal
privacy that separates us from everything else. On the contrary, sex joins us to the world. If it doesn't carry us into love
for what it joins us to, then it carries us into disrespect, damage, and loneliness. Thinking of the human family's "ec-
static moment, the sexual choice of man and woman," and
of the perils of that moment, William Butler Yeats wrote
that "the great sculptors, painters, and poets are there that
instinct may find its lamp." The lamp that human culture
holds up for the guidance of human instinct is something
that we too must think about. For our connection to nature
is never theoretical. We work it out daily in the most insis-
tently practical ways. In dealing with our own fertility and
its consequences, we are not just carrying on personal or private "relationships." We are establishing one of the fundamental terms of our humanity and our connection to the
world.

For clarification, we can turn once again to those opposed
historical themes (and psychologies) of boomer and sticker.
Boomers, as Wallace Stegner understood them, are people
who expect or demand that the world conform to their desires. They either succeed and thus damage the world, or they
fail and thus damage their families and themselves.

In the *New Yorker* for December 27, 1993, Daphne Merkin characterized as follows "the postmodern view of connubial love":

> To live with a man or a woman on an ongoing, intimate basis is to grow jaded, weary of the imaginative possibilities; at some point our husbands and wives fail to live up to a long-ago sensed potential. They become to us who they have become to themselves, and it is hard to envision them as promising more than they currently yield.

Ms. Merkin's description conforms exactly to the understanding of boomer desire that we find in *The Big Rock Candy Mountain*: "Why remain in one dull plot of earth when Heaven was reachable, was touchable, was just over there?" There is nothing new or "postmodern" in Ms. Merkin's description; it describes, in fact, the psychology of the Spanish gold seekers of the sixteenth century and their countless followers until now. The boomer's mind operates outside all restraints of culture and principle. Just as tragically, it operates outside history; it does not remember experience. It deals with all of its subjects on the basis of the crudest sort of economic metaphor. Any person, place, or thing is understood as a mine having a limited "yield"; when the yield falls below expectation, it is time to move on. It is easy to see that the boomer's mind must be equally destructive of nature and of humanity—hard on landscapes and on spouses, hard on children and other small creatures.

We have, in fact, no right to ask the world to conform to our desires. Sooner or later, if we hope to grow up, we have to confront the opposite imperative: that our rights and the realization of our desires are limited by human nature, by human community, and by the nature of the places in which we live. If we can accept our world's real limits and the responsibilities that protect our authentic rights, if we can unite affection and fidelity, if we can keep instinct and light together, then (as our tradition teaches) we may hope to transcend our limits, so that our life may grow in generosity, love, grace, and beauty without end.

POSTSCRIPT

The issue of abortion is now so volatile that it is difficult to contain satisfactorily in an essay about something else—as I have shown here. I have more that I need to say. And yet it may be that one should write of abortion *only* in an essay about something else. It is not a subject unto itself; treating it as such leads to further trouble. It is a subject, on the contrary, that appears to call always for greater complexity and consistency of thought.

It cannot, for example, be very safely thought about from a position of assumed immunity. We humans must think about our evils from the inside, because we must think about our condition from the inside. That I believe abortion to be wrong does not mean that I cannot imagine situations in which I would support a woman's decision to have an abortion—or in which I would have an abortion, if I were a woman, or perform an abortion, if I were a doctor. Because we are human, we don't have the happiness of choosing always between good and evil. Sometimes we must choose between two evils, and I don't recommend turning away from anybody in that predicament. Because our life does not always offer us clean-cut choices between good and evil, we are going to need forgiveness. And I believe in the possibility of forgiveness, as I believe in the possibility of just remorse.

We are nevertheless entrusted with the care of our fellow human creatures. If abortion is wrong, as I believe, it is wrong because it excludes some of our fellow humans from our care. But to think that abortion is wrong is to risk dangerous oversimplification if we cannot follow our thought to its logical conclusion. If we cannot justify violence to unborn human beings, then how can we justify violence to those who are born, or to the world that they are born into?

The issue ultimately turns on one question: Is a human fetus a human being? I believe that it is. Anybody who believes that it is not must say what else on earth it might be.

Health Is
Membership

Delivered as a speech at a conference, "Spirituality and Healing," at Louisville, Kentucky, on October 17, 1994.

I

FROM OUR CONSTANT and increasing concerns about health, you can tell how seriously diseased we are. Health, as we may remember from at least some of the days of our youth, is at once wholeness and a kind of unconsciousness. Disease (dis-ease), on the contrary, makes us conscious not only of the state of our health but of the division of our bodies and our world into parts.

The word "health," in fact, comes from the same Indo-

European root as "heal," "whole," and "holy." To be healthy is literally to be whole; to heal is to make whole. I don't think mortal healers should be credited with the power to make holy. But I have no doubt that such healers are properly obliged to acknowledge and respect the holiness embodied in all creatures, or that our healing involves the preservation in us of the spirit and the breath of God.

If we were lucky enough as children to be surrounded by grown-ups who loved us, then our sense of wholeness is not just the sense of completeness in ourselves but also is the sense of belonging to others and to our place; it is an unconscious awareness of community, of having in common. It may be that this double sense of singular integrity and of communal belonging is our personal standard of health for as long as we live. Anyhow, we seem to know instinctively that health is not divided.

Of course, growing up and growing older as fallen creatures in a fallen world can only instruct us painfully in division and disintegration. This is the stuff of consciousness and experience. But if our culture works in us as it should, then we do not age merely into disintegration and division, but that very experience begins our education, leading us into knowledge of wholeness and of holiness. I am describing here the story of Job, of Lazarus, of the lame man at the pool of Bethesda, of Milton's Samson, of King Lear. If our culture works in us as it should, our experience is balanced by education; we are led out of our lonely suffering and are made whole.

In the present age of the world, disintegration and division, isolation and suffering seem to have overwhelmed us. The balance between experience and education has been overthrown; we are lost in experience, and so-called education is leading us nowhere. We have diseases aplenty. As if that were not enough, we are suffering an almost universal hypochondria. Half the energy of the medical industry, one suspects, may now be devoted to "examinations" or "tests"— to see if, though apparently well, we may not be latently or insidiously diseased.

If you are going to deal with the issue of health in the modern world, you are going to have to deal with much absurdity. It is not clear, for example, why death should increasingly be looked upon as a curable disease, an abnormality, by a society that increasingly looks upon life as insupportably painful and/or meaningless. Even more startling is the realization that the modern medical industry faithfully imitates disease in the way that it isolates us and parcels us out. If, for example, intense and persistent pain causes you to pay attention only to your stomach, then you must leave home, community, and family and go to a sometimes distant clinic or hospital, where you will be cared for by a specialist who will pay attention only to your stomach.

Or consider the announcement by the Associated Press on February 9, 1994, that "the incidence of cancer is up among all ages, and researchers speculated that environmental exposure to cancer-causing substances other than cigarettes may be partly to blame." This bit of news is offered as a surprise, never mind that the environment (so called) has been known to be polluted and toxic for many years. The blame obviously falls on that idiotic term "the environment," which refers to a world that surrounds us but is presumably different from us and distant from us. Our laboratories have proved long ago that cigarette smoke gets inside us, but if "the environment" surrounds us, how does *it* wind up inside us? So much for division as a working principle of health.

This, plainly, is a view of health that is severely reductive. It is, to begin with, almost fanatically individualistic. The body is seen as a defective or potentially defective machine, singular, solitary, and displaced, without love, solace, or pleasure. Its health excludes unhealthy cigarettes but does not exclude unhealthy food, water, and air. One may presumably be healthy in a disintegrated family or community or in a destroyed or poisoned ecosystem.

So far, I have been implying my beliefs at every turn. Now I had better state them openly.

I take literally the statement in the Gospel of John that God loves the world. I believe that the world was created and approved by love, that it subsists, coheres, and endures by love, and that, insofar as it is redeemable, it can be redeemed only by love. I believe that divine love, incarnate and indwelling in the world, summons the world always toward wholeness, which ultimately is reconciliation and atonement with God.

I believe that health is wholeness. For many years I have returned again and again to the work of the English agriculturist Sir Albert Howard, who said, in *The Soil and Health*, that "the whole problem of health in soil, plant, animal, and man [is] one great subject."

I am moreover a Luddite, in what I take to be the true and appropriate sense. I am not "against technology" so much as I am for community. When the choice is between the health of a community and technological innovation, I choose the health of the community. I would unhesitatingly destroy a machine before I would allow the machine to destroy my community.

I believe that the community—in the fullest sense: a place and all its creatures—is the smallest unit of health and that to speak of the health of an isolated individual is a contradiction in terms.

We speak now of "spirituality and healing" as if the only way to render a proper religious respect to the body is somehow to treat it "spiritually." It could be argued just as appropriately (and perhaps less dangerously) that the way to respect the body fully is to honor fully its materiality. In saying this, I intend no reduction. I do not doubt the reality of the experience and knowledge we call "spiritual" any more than I doubt the reality of so-called physical experience and knowledge; I recognize the rough utility of these terms. But I strongly doubt the advantage, and even the possibility, of separating these two realities.

What I'm arguing against here is not complexity or mystery but dualism. I would like to purge my own mind and language of such terms as "spiritual," "physical," "metaphysical," and "transcendental"—all of which imply that the Creation is divided into "levels" that can readily be peeled apart and judged by human beings. I believe that the Creation is one continuous fabric comprehending simultaneously what we mean by "spirit" and what we mean by "matter."

Our bodies are involved in the world. Their needs and desires and pleasures are physical. Our bodies hunger and thirst, yearn toward other bodies, grow tired and seek rest, rise up rested, eager to exert themselves. All these desires may be satisfied with honor to the body and its maker, but only if much else besides the individual body is brought into consideration. We have long known that individual desires must not be made the standard of their own satisfaction. We must consider the body's manifold connections to other bodies and to the world. The body, "fearfully and wonderfully made," is ultimately mysterious both in itself and in its dependences. Our bodies live, the Bible says, by the spirit and the breath of God, but it does not say how this is so. We are not going to *know* about this.

The distinction between the physical and the spiritual is, I believe, false. A much more valid distinction, and one that we need urgently to learn to make, is that between the organic and the mechanical. To argue this—as I am going to do—puts me in the minority, I know, but it does not make me unique. In *The Idea of a Christian Society*, T. S. Eliot wrote, "We may say that religion, as distinguished from modern paganism, implies a life in conformity with nature. It may be observed that the natural life and the supernatural life have a conformity to each other which neither has with the mechanistic life."

Still, I wonder if our persistent wish to deal spiritually with physical things does not come either from the feeling that physical things are "low" and unworthy or from the fear, especially when speaking of affection, that "physical" will be taken to mean "sexual."

The *New York Review of Books* of February 3, 1994, for example, carried a review of the correspondence of William and Henry James along with a photograph of the two brothers standing together with William's arm around Henry's shoulders. Apropos of this picture, the reviewer, John Bayley, wrote that "their closeness of affection was undoubted and even took on occasion a quasi-physical form." It is Mr. Bayley's qualifier, "quasi-physical," that sticks in one's mind. What can he have meant by it? Is this prurience masquerading as squeamishness, or vice versa? Does Mr. Bayley feel a need to assure his psychologically sophisticated readers that even though these brothers touched one another familiarly, they were not homosexual lovers?

The phrase involves at least some version of the old dualism of spirit and body or mind and body that has caused us so much suffering and trouble and that raises such troubling questions for anybody who is interested in health. If you love your brother and if you and your brother are living creatures, how could your love for him not be physical? Not spiritual or mental only, not "quasi-physical," but physical. How could you not take a simple pleasure in putting your arm around him?

Out of the same dualism comes our confusion about the body's proper involvement in the world. People seriously interested in health will finally have to question our society's long-standing goals of convenience and effortlessness. What is the point of "labor saving" if by making work effortless we make it poor, and if by doing poor work we weaken our bodies and lose conviviality and health?

We are now pretty clearly involved in a crisis of health, one of the wonders of which is its immense profitability both to those who cause it and to those who propose to cure it. That the illness may prove incurable, except by catastrophe, is suggested by our economic dependence on it. Think, for example, of how readily our solutions become problems and our cures pollutants. To cure one disease, we need another. The causes, of course, are numerous and complicated, but all of them, I think, can be traced back to the old idea that our bodies are not very important except when they give us pleasure (usually, now, to somebody's profit) or when they hurt (now, almost invariably, to somebody's profit).

This dualism inevitably reduces physical reality, and it does so by removing its mystery from it, by dividing it absolutely from what dualistic thinkers have understood as spiritual or mental reality.

A reduction that is merely theoretical might be harmless enough, I suppose, but theories find ways of getting into action. The theory of the relative unimportance of physical reality has put itself into action by means of a metaphor by which the body (along with the world itself) is understood as a machine. According to this metaphor—which is now in constant general use—the human heart, for example, is no longer understood as the center of our emotional life or even as an organ that pumps; it is understood as "a pump," having somewhat the same function as a fuel pump in an automobile.

If the body is a machine for living and working, then it must follow that the mind is a machine for thinking. The "progress" here is the reduction of mind to brain and then of brain to computer. This reduction implies and requires the reduction of knowledge to "information." It requires, in fact, the reduction of everything to numbers and mathematical operations.

This metaphor of the machine bears heavily upon the question of what we mean by health and by healing. The problem is that like any metaphor, it is accurate only in some respects. A girl is only in some respects like a red rose; a heart is only in some respects like a pump. This means that a metaphor must be controlled by a sort of humorous intelligence, always mindful of the exact limits within which the comparison is meaningful. When a metaphor begins to control intelligence, as this one of the machine has done for a long time, then we must look for costly distortions and absurdities.

Of course, the body in most ways is not at all like a machine. Like all living creatures and unlike a machine, the body is not formally self-contained; its boundaries and outlines are not so exactly fixed. The body alone is not, properly speaking, a body. Divided from its sources of air, food, drink, clothing, shelter, and companionship, a body is, properly speaking, a cadaver, whereas a machine by itself, shut down or out of fuel, is still a machine. Merely as an organism (leaving aside issues of mind and spirit) the body lives and moves and has its being, minute by minute, by an interinvolvement with other bodies and other creatures, living and unliving, that is too complex to diagram or describe. It is, moreover, under the influence of thought and feeling. It does not live by "fuel" alone.

A mind, probably, is even less like a computer than a body is like a machine. As far as I am able to understand it, a mind is not even much like a brain. Insofar as it is usable for thought, for the association of thought with feeling, for the association of thoughts and feelings with words, for the connections between words and things, words and acts, thought and memory, a mind seems to be in constant need of reminding. A mind unreminded would be no mind at all. This phenomenon of reminding shows the extensiveness of mind—how intricately it is involved with sensation, emotion, memory, tradition, communal life, known landscapes, and so on. How you could locate a mind within its full extent, among all its subjects and necessities, I don't know, but obviously it cannot be located within a brain or a computer.

To see better what a mind is (or is not), we might consider the difference between what we mean by knowledge and what the computer now requires us to mean by "information." Knowledge refers to the ability to do or say the right thing at the right time; we would not speak of somebody who does the wrong thing at the wrong time as "knowledgeable." People who perform well as musicians, athletes, teachers, or farmers are people of knowledge. And such examples tell us much about the nature of knowledge. Knowledge is formal, and it informs speech and action. It is instantaneous; it is present and available when and where it is needed.

"Information," which once meant that which forms or fashions from within, now means merely "data." However organized this data may be, it is not shapely or formal or in the true sense in-forming. It is not present where it is needed; if you have to "access" it, you don't have it. Whereas knowledge moves and forms acts, information is inert. You cannot imagine a debater or a quarterback or a musician performing by "accessing information." A computer chock full of such information is no more admirable than a head or a book chock full of it.

The difference, then, between information and knowledge is something like the difference between a dictionary and somebody's language.

Where the art and science of healing are concerned, the machine metaphor works to enforce a division that falsifies the process of healing because it falsifies the nature of the creature needing to be healed. If the body is a machine, then its diseases can be healed by a sort of mechanical tinkering, without reference to anything outside the body itself. This applies, with obvious differences, to the mind; people are assumed to be individually sane or insane. And so we return to the utter anomaly of a creature that is healthy within itself.

The modern hospital, where most of us receive our strictest lessons in the nature of industrial medicine, undoubtedly does well at surgery and other procedures that permit the body and its parts to be treated as separate things. But when you try to think of it as a place of healing—of reconnecting and making whole—then the hospital reveals the disarray of the medical industry's thinking about health.

In healing, the body is restored to itself. It begins to live again by its own powers and instincts, to the extent that it can do so. To the extent that it can do so, it goes free of drugs and mechanical helps. Its appetites return. It relishes food and rest. The patient is restored to family and friends, home and community and work.

This process has a certain naturalness and inevitability, like that by which a child grows up, but industrial medicine seems to grasp it only tentatively and awkwardly. For example, any ordinary person would assume that a place of healing would put a premium upon rest, but hospitals are notoriously difficult to sleep in. They are noisy all night, and the routine interventions go on relentlessly. The body is treated as a machine that does not need to rest.

You would think also that a place dedicated to healing and health would make much of food. But here is where the disconnections of the industrial system and the displacement of industrial humanity are most radical. Sir Albert Howard saw accurately that the issue of human health is inseparable from the health of the soil, and he saw too that we humans must responsibly occupy our place in the cycle of birth, growth, maturity, death, and decay, which is the health of the world. Aside from our own mortal involvement, food is our fundamental connection to that cycle. But probably most of the

complaints you hear about hospitals have to do with the
food, which, according to the testimony I have heard, tends
to range from unappetizing to sickening. Food is treated as
another unpleasant substance to inject. And this is a shame.
For in addition to the obvious nutritional link between food
and health, food can be a pleasure. People who are sick are
often troubled or depressed, and mealtimes offer three opportunities a day when patients could easily be offered something to look forward to. Nothing is more pleasing or
heartening than a plate of nourishing, tasty, beautiful food
artfully and lovingly prepared. Anything less is unhealthy, as
well as a desecration.

Why should rest and food and ecological health not be the
basic principles of our art and science of healing? Is it because
the basic principles already are technology and drugs? Are
we confronting some fundamental incompatibility between
mechanical efficiency and organic health? I don't know. I
only know that sleeping in a hospital is like sleeping in a
factory and that the medical industry makes only the most
tenuous connection between health and food and no connection between health and the soil. Industrial medicine is
as little interested in ecological health as is industrial agriculture.

A further problem, and an equally serious one, is that illness, in addition to being a bodily disaster, is now also an
economic disaster. This is so whether or not the patient is in-
sured. It is a disaster for us all, all the time, because we all
know that personally or collectively, we cannot continue to
pay for cures that continue to get more expensive. The eco-

nomic disturbance that now inundates the problem of illness may turn out to be the profoundest illness of all. How can we get well if we are worried sick about money?

I wish it were not the fate of this essay to be filled with questions, but questions now seem the inescapable end of any line of thought about health and healing. Here are several more:

1. Can our present medical industry produce an adequate definition of health? My own guess is that it cannot do so. Like industrial agriculture, industrial medicine has depended increasingly on specialist methodology, mechanical technology, and chemicals; thus, its point of reference has become more and more its own technical prowess and less and less the health of creatures and habitats. I don't expect this problem to be solved in the universities, which have never addressed, much less solved, the problem of health in agriculture. And I don't expect it to be solved by the government.

2. How can cheapness be included in the criteria of medical experimentation and performance? And why has it not been included before now? I believe that the problem here is again that of the medical industry's fixation on specialization, technology, and chemistry. As a result, the modern "health care system" has become a way of marketing industrial products, exactly like modern agriculture, impoverishing those who pay and enriching those who are paid. It is, in other words, an industry such as industries have always been.

3. Why is it that medical strictures and recommendations so often work in favor of food processors and against food producers? Why, for example, do we so strongly favor the pas-

teurization of milk to health and cleanliness in milk production? (Gene Logsdon correctly says that the motive here "is monopoly, not consumer health.")

4. Why do we so strongly prefer a fat-free or a germ-free diet to a chemical-free diet? Why does the medical industry strenuously oppose the use of tobacco, yet complacently accept the massive use of antibiotics and other drugs in meat animals and of poisons on food crops? How much longer can it cling to the superstition of bodily health in a polluted world?

5. How can adequate medical and health care, including disease prevention, be included in the structure and economy of a community? How, for example, can a community and its doctors be included in the same culture, the same knowledge, and the same fate, so that they will live as fellow citizens, sharers in a common wealth, members of one another?

II

IT IS CLEAR by now that this essay cannot hope to be complete; the problems are too large and my knowledge too small. What I have to offer is an association of thoughts and questions wandering somewhat at random and somewhat lost within the experience of modern diseases and the often bewildering industry that undertakes to cure them. In my ignorance and bewilderment, I am fairly representative of those who go, or go with loved ones, to doctors' offices and hospitals. What I have written so far comes from my various efforts to make as much sense as I can of that experience. But now I had better turn to the experience itself.

On January 3, 1994, my brother John had a severe heart attack while he was out by himself on his farm, moving a feed trough. He managed to get to the house and telephone a friend, who sent the emergency rescue squad.

The rescue squad and the emergency room staff at a local hospital certainly saved my brother's life. He was later moved to a hospital in Louisville, where a surgeon performed a double-bypass operation on his heart. After three weeks John returned home. He still has a life to live and work to do. He has been restored to himself and to the world.

He and those who love him have a considerable debt to the medical industry, as represented by two hospitals, several doctors and nurses, many drugs and many machines. This is a debt that I cheerfully acknowledge. But I am obliged to say also that my experience of the hospital during John's stay was troubled by much conflict of feeling and a good many unresolved questions, and I know that I am not alone in this.

In the hospital what I will call the world of love meets the world of efficiency—the world, that is, of specialization, machinery, and abstract procedure. Or, rather, I should say that these two worlds come together in the hospital but do not meet. During those weeks when John was in the hospital, it seemed to me that he had come from the world of love and that the family members, neighbors, and friends who at various times were there with him came there to represent that world and to preserve his connection with it. It seemed to me that the hospital was another kind of world altogether.

When I said early in this essay that we live in a world that was created and exists and is redeemable by love, I did not mean to sentimentalize it. For this is also a fallen world. It involves error and disease, ignorance and partiality, sin and death. If this world is a place where we may learn of our involvement in immortal love, as I believe it is, still such learning is only possible here because that love involves us so inescapably in the limits, sufferings, and sorrows of mortality.

Like divine love, earthly love seeks plenitude; it longs for the full membership to be present and to be joined. Unlike divine love, earthly love does not have the power, the knowledge, or the will to achieve what it longs for. The story of human love on this earth is a story by which this love reveals and even validates itself by its failures to be complete and comprehensive and effective enough. When this love enters a hospital, it brings with it a terrifying history of defeat, but it comes nevertheless confident of itself, for its existence and the power of its longing have been proved over and over again even by its defeat. In the face of illness, the threat of death, and death itself, it insists unabashedly on its own presence, understanding by its persistence through defeat that it is superior to whatever happens.

The world of efficiency ignores both loves, earthly and divine, because by definition it must reduce experience to computation, particularity to abstraction, and mystery to a small comprehensibility. Efficiency, in our present sense of the word, allies itself inevitably with machinery, as Neil Postman demonstrates in his useful book, *Technopoly*. "Machines," he says, "eliminate complexity, doubt, and ambiguity. They work swiftly, they are standardized, and they provide us with numbers that you can see and calculate with." To reason, the advantages are obvious, and probably no reasonable person would wish to reject them out of hand.

And yet love obstinately answers that no loved one is standardized. A body, love insists, is neither a spirit nor a machine; it is not a picture, a diagram, a chart, a graph, an anatomy; it is not an explanation; it is not a law. It is precisely and uniquely what it is. It belongs to the world of love, which is a world of living creatures, natural orders and cycles, many small, fragile lights in the dark.

In dealing with problems of agriculture, I had thought much about the difference between creatures and machines. But I had never so clearly understood and felt that difference as when John was in recovery after his heart surgery, when he was attached to many machines and was dependent for breath on a respirator. It was impossible then not to see that the breathing of a machine, like all machine work, is unvarying, an oblivious regularity, whereas the breathing of a creature is ever changing, exquisitely responsive to events both inside and outside the body, to thoughts and emotions. A machine makes breaths as a machine makes buttons, all the same, but every breath of a creature is itself a creature, like no other, inestimably precious.

Logically, in plenitude some things ought to be expendable. Industrial economics has always believed this: abundance justifies waste. This is one of the dominant superstitions of

American history—and of the history of colonialism everywhere. Expendability is also an assumption of the world of efficiency, which is why that world deals so compulsively in percentages of efficacy and safety.

But this sort of logic is absolutely alien to the world of love. To the claim that a certain drug or procedure would save 99 percent of all cancer patients or that a certain pollutant would be safe for 99 percent of a population, love, unembarrassed, would respond, "What about the one percent?"

There is nothing rational or perhaps even defensible about this, but it is nonetheless one of the strongest strands of our religious tradition—it is probably the most essential strand—according to which a shepherd, owning a hundred sheep and having lost one, does not say, "I have saved 99 percent of my sheep," but rather, "I have lost one," and he goes and searches for the one. And if the sheep in that parable may seem to be only a metaphor, then go on to the Gospel of Luke, where the principle is flatly set forth again and where the sparrows stand not for human beings but for all creatures: "Are not five sparrows sold for two farthings, and not one of them is forgotten before God?" And John Donne had in mind a sort of equation and not a mere metaphor when he wrote, "If a clod be washed away by the sea, Europe is the less, as well as if a promontory were, as well as if a manor of thy friend's or of thine own were. Any man's death diminishes me."

It is reassuring to see ecology moving toward a similar idea of the order of things. If an ecosystem loses one of its native species, we now know that we cannot speak of it as itself minus one species. An ecosystem minus one species is a different ecosystem. Just so, each of us is made by—or, one might better say, made as—a set of unique associations with unique persons, places, and things. The world of love does not admit the principle of the interchangeability of parts.

When John was in intensive care after his surgery, his wife, Carol, was standing by his bed, grieving and afraid. Wanting to reassure her, the nurse said, "Nothing is happening to him that doesn't happen to everybody."

And Carol replied, "I'm not everybody's wife."

In the world of love, things separated by efficiency and specialization strive to come back together. And yet love must confront death, and accept it, and learn from it. Only in confronting death can earthly love learn its true extent, its immortality. Any definition of health that is not silly must include death. The world of love includes death, suffers it, and triumphs over it. The world of efficiency is defeated by death; at death, all its instruments and procedures stop. The world of love continues, and of this grief is the proof.

In the hospital, love cannot forget death. But like love, death is in the hospital but not of it. Like love, fear and grief feel out of place in the hospital. How could they be included in its efficient procedures and mechanisms? Where a clear, small order is fervently maintained, fear and grief bring the threat of large disorder.

And so these two incompatible worlds might also be designated by the terms "amateur" and "professional"—amateur, in the literal sense of lover, one who participates for love; and professional in the modern sense of one who performs highly specialized or technical procedures for pay. The amateur is excluded from the professional "field."

For the amateur, in the hospital or in almost any other encounter with the medical industry, the overriding experience is that of being excluded from knowledge—of being unable, in other words, to make or participate in anything resembling an "informed decision." Of course, whether doctors make informed decisions in the hospital is a matter of debate. For in the hospital even the professionals are involved in experience; experimentation has been left far behind. Experience, as all amateurs know, is not predictable, and in experience there are no replications or "controls"; there is nothing with which to compare the result. Once one decision has been made, we have destroyed the opportunity to know what would have happened if another decision had been made. That is to say that medicine is an exact science until applied; application involves intuition, a sense of probability, "gut feeling," guesswork, and error.

In medicine, as in many modern disciplines, the amateur is divided from the professional by perhaps unbridgeable differences of knowledge and of language. An "informed decision" is really not even imaginable for most medical patients and their families, who have no competent understanding of either the patient's illness or the recommended medical or surgical procedure. Moreover, patients and their families are not likely to know the doctor, the surgeon, or any of the other people on whom the patient's life will depend. In the hospital, amateurs are more than likely to be proceeding entirely upon faith—and this is a peculiar and scary faith, for it must be placed not in a god but in mere people, mere procedures, mere chemicals, and mere machines.

It was only after my brother had been taken into surgery, I think, that the family understood the extremity of this deed of faith. We had decided   or John had decided and we had concurred—on the basis of the best advice available. But once he was separated from us, we felt the burden of our ignorance. We had not known what we were doing, and one of our difficulties now was the feeling that we had utterly given him up to what we did not know. John himself spoke out of this sense of abandonment and helplessness in the intensive care unit, when he said, "I don't know what they're going to do to me or for me or with me."

As we waited and reports came at long intervals from the operating room, other realizations followed. We realized that under the circumstances, we could not be told the truth. We would not know, ever, the worries and surprises that came to the surgeon during his work. We would not know the critical moments or the fears. If the surgeon did any part of his work ineptly or made a mistake, we would not know it. We realized, moreover, that if we were told the truth, we would have no way of knowing that the truth was what it was.

We realized that when the emissaries from the operating room assured us that everything was "normal" or "routine," they were referring to the procedure and not the patient. Even as amateurs—perhaps *because* we were amateurs—we knew that what was happening was not normal or routine for John or for us.

That these two worlds are so radically divided does not mean that people cannot cross between them. I do not know how an amateur can cross over into the professional world; that does not seem very probable. But that professional people can cross back into the amateur world, I know from much evidence. During John's stay in the hospital there were many moments in which doctors and nurses—especially nurses!—allowed or caused the professional relationship to become a meeting between two human beings, and these moments were invariably moving.

The most moving, to me, happened in the waiting room during John's surgery. From time to time a nurse from the operating room would come in to tell Carol what was happening. Carol, from politeness or bravery or both, always stood to receive the news, which always left us somewhat encouraged and somewhat doubtful. Carol's difficulty was that she had to suffer the ordeal not only as a wife but as one who had been a trained nurse. She knew, from her own education and experience, in how limited a sense open-heart surgery could be said to be normal or routine.

Finally, toward the end of our wait, two nurses came in. The operation, they said, had been a success. They explained again what had been done. And then they said that after the completion of the bypasses, the surgeon had found it necessary to insert a "balloon pump" into the aorta to assist the heart. This possibility had never been mentioned, nobody was prepared for it, and Carol was sorely disappointed and upset. The two young women attempted to reassure her, mainly by repeating things they had already said. And then there was a long moment when they just looked at her. It was such a look as parents sometimes give to a sick or suffering child, when they themselves have begun to need the comfort they are trying to give.

And then one of the nurses said, "Do you need a hug?"

"Yes," Carol said.

And the nurse gave her a hug.

Which brings us to a starting place.

p 7 6   Importance of faith